ARCHITECTURE
A VISUAL HISTORY

Petronas Towers, Kuala Lumpur, Malaysia (1997 AD)

Cesar Pelli

Photographer: Richard Bryant/8000:200

ARCHITECTURE
A VISUAL HISTORY

JAMES NEAL

This edition published by Barnes and Noble Inc.,
by arrangement with PRC Publishing Ltd.

2004 Barnes and Noble Books

M 10 9 8 7 6 5 4 3 2 1

ISBN 0-7607-5519-1

Produced by PRC Publishing Limited
The Chrysalis Building
Bramley Road, London W10 6SP
An imprint of Chrysalis Books Group plc

Printed in China

CONTENTS

INTRODUCTION

THE NATURE OF ARCHITECTURE

Is architecture an art or a science? This is not an easy question to answer, because the two elements combine in all buildings: without science buildings are unlikely to have any structural permanence; if they lack art, people would not find them beautiful enough to allow them to remain over the years. Since the appreciation of architecture tends to be based on a building's form rather than its function, it is judged visually — on its artistic merit — and so the observer inevitably makes personal subjective judgements. Based on their own view of what is beautiful and on their received information of what others judge to be beautiful, the observer interprets, misinterprets and reinterprets architecture. What one person may think is beautiful, the next finds repulsive: it is this subjective decision-making that encourages the very creativity that has influenced architects over the centuries.

Much of our concept of architecture is based on received information: over the years the architecture of the past has been categorized, labeled and had judgement passed on it. But, in spite of this process, deciding on a comprehensive and definitive list of the important architecture of the world is difficult, if not impossible. Even if the accepted guides to what exemplifies a style are followed closely, there will always be arguments as to which specific building defines that moment. Certainly, the photographs chosen for this book will not always be of these defining buildings in everyone's eyes. To cover photographically the whole spectrum of architecture from the Pyramids of Egypt to the Millennium Dome in London, other criteria come into play: for example, which structures have best survived the predations of humans and time and so remain still to be photographed; which structures cannot be photographed because of their position or environment; and, more prosaically, which structures have the best photographic coverage — a criterion that is also based on a subjective choice.

Naturally formed shelters often became the basis for early shelters, especially in regions where the weather was extreme.

What is evident from the photographs in this book are the continual themes and principal methods that are the foundation of architecture. The themes and principles that an architect learns from close study of the past generate new ideas and interpretations. Architects require external influences to guide them in their designs: few, if any, can create in a vacuum. Even if an architect were to blatantly disregard all the architecture of the past, at some point they would have had to examine and understand its very nature to be so dismissive. It is only the advent of new technology that can allow such a quantum jump in design — much as happened in the 20th century. Perhaps the technologies of the new millennium will allow architects to break with the constrictions of the past and allow the observer to view and, ultimately, interact with architecture on an entirely new level. Until such a time we are left to view architecture, as we know it today.

The principles of design, creativity and ideology are fundamental to the overall nature of architecture. Whatever the intended function of a building, the architect has always had to use a creative process in the design. Often this stems from an ideology, sometimes in the face of adverse objections and criticism from others. The effect on the users and observers is not always easy to grasp, and nor should it be. Architecture, whether good or bad, is one of the fundamental influences on our daily activities, a major factor in how we go about our lives. It is the ultimate mark of confidence in the power and culture of a society; from the Pyramids of Giza to the great palaces and cathedrals of Europe or to their modern equivalents, the museums and municipal buildings of our cities.

The economic power of a society and its social behavior has always been expressed in the architecture of its public spaces — as here in Las Vegas.

Interpreting the influence architecture has upon us is difficult. It comes as a surprise to find how, today, over-heated arguments rage over the decision to destroy or preserve old buildings. Seldom can there have been a time when so many people have so clearly and expressively voiced their opinions on architecture. The increased profile of architecture through the television, books and the media has helped create this environment, but it has also had a negative effect: the profile and influence of the architect has diminished. The once central role of the architect and their architecture as a catalyst for the evolution of society is no longer straightforward. The once noble profession is now, especially in Great Britain, the focus of contempt, and simply seen as the public exploration of an inflated ego. Regardless of how we view the role of the architect and his/her profession, the focus for the users and observers should be on the by-product of their imaginations.

The complexity of architecture means that, unlike any other art form, it has to be judged in the context of the era in which it was built. Not only has the surrounding vernacular buildings to be considered, but also the socio-political climate at the time of the structure's conception through to its completion. Architecture, in other words, does not travel, unlike a painting or a sculpture that are rarely specific to one place. Fine art can often be isolated from external influences so that it can be viewed in its purest form; it does not have to contend with the burdens of functionality or physics, factors that can alter designers' intentions considerably. This duality of function and form is one that has caused endless debate over the years. Whether or not you hold true the opinion "form follows function," it is the "form" that is primarily scrutinized. Rightly or wrongly, it is the look of a building that is often the key to its success, often in spite of flaws in the usability. It is the visuals that also determine in which stylistic category we place a building, even if the architect envisioned it differently.

What distinguishes a style? This question is frequently asked but seldom can a definitive answer be given; every architect draws his inspiration from a myriad of influences and no two will be the same. Similarly an architect will not always use the same combination of influences again. Like any art form, architecture is continually evolving.

The influences on any particular style come from diverse sources, often unrelated but seldom separated. The political environment in which the building was designed plays one of the greatest roles — because of planning legislation or the stronger socio-political context of the environment. Many styles have evolved out of opposition to the existing political position, as a reaction to what the proponents see as repressive societies. The suppression of the arts — and the free thinkers who create it — is usually the first step of an extreme political regime. Despite this, the involvement of politics with architecture can often lead the intense creativity and the development of influential styles and movements — sometimes as result of repression but also as a product of patronage. Architectural movements encompass a variety of artistic fields, including not only fine art but philosophy as well. The prominence of a particular style or movement over another is often solely due to political patrons.

Throughout the ages there have been key figureheads within each movement that act as spokesmen for a particular style. These figureheads take the limelight, but often it is others that show a greater understanding of the style or develop it. Although sequential styles can be very similar and frequently stem from the same influences, the difference in the interpretation of these influences can be vastly different. Those reacting against prominent fashions will try to go against the grain, not only to forward their own way of thinking, but often also to elevate their own standing in the artistic and commercial fields. Today we are in an unenviable position where large corporations dictate styles through their choice of architects; usually, this means those who follow safe and inoffensive styles. This has had a two-fold, almost Darwinian effect on architecture — it suppresses many fresh ideas, but at the same time ensures that any new style that survives is stronger for the birth pains. As we enter the 21st Century, a few brave corporations and patrons are beginning to employ the services of influential architects who are, or have recently been seen, as the avant-garde of their profession.

The new millennium should bring new exciting architecture, but what we can be sure is that future styles will rely on what has gone in the past, as building blocks to a new vision. It is only the advent of new technology, and the extent to which man is willing to make use of it, that will lead to developments that owe little to previous sources of inspiration and more to the high end of science and even science fiction. To understand today we have to understand yesterday; to understand tomorrow we will have to wait and see . . .

The ancient Egyptians celebrated the life of the rich and powerful leaders of their time by immortalising them in cities of the dead.

ANCIENT EGYPT

Variations in style within the long history of Egypt are minimal; temple façades with over a thousand years between completion dates show similar principles and details. What remains of ancient Egyptian architecture are mainly the massive monuments and temples to the ruling classes — pure homages to the power and divine greatness of a pharaoh. Once the form of their buildings had achieved its optimum functional level, it remained the same; permanence was symbolized and reinforced by repetition.

The earliest permanent cities that developed in this region were designed for the dead: streets of tombs laid out in a grid pattern modeled like small houses. Inhabitable cities first arose to house the numerous building workers of the public structures such as the pyramids. The Nile was the lifeline for Ancient Egypt, not only providing trade routes and lush farmlands, but also the baked mud of the harvested fields literally gave the essential building blocks for these early houses. It was soon discovered that greater structural stability could be found by molding and strengthening the blocks, it was these early materials that were used in the first major monumental tombs; a rectangular based mound with battered walls known as a mastabas.

Entrances to the pyramids were kept a secret and located at unspecified distances to the north of the tombs.

Although we associate stone work with Ancient Egypt, it was the Egyptians' use of mud and reeds in the vernacular architecture of the Nile valley that formulated the techniques they would require to build in stone. It was the reeds that were used as the basic framework for structures: these were bundled together to form primitive columns and lintels that supported flat clay roofs. The pressure of the roof gave the columns the distinctive "gorge" cornice that was later reproduced in stone. Other features that first showed in vernacular structures were passed down to the stone constructions; the horizontal binders and angled bundles became the rolled molding of stone cornices and angled walls. Another important decorative characteristic of Egyptian architecture, hieroglyphics, are also thought to have derived from the pictures scratched on the mud walls.

But it is the iconistic structures of Egypt, the pyramids, that exhibit the qualities that make the architecture of this region special. Almost every edifice in Ancient Egypt was constructed to plans in which astronomical calculations played every bit as large a part as the aesthetics. Put quite simply, the Egyptians were creating heaven on earth. This can be clearly seen in the pyramids of Khufu whose positional plan is directly and accurately translated to that of the constellation we call Orion's Belt. While most of the pyramids were built purely as tombs for pharaohs to gain immortality by preserving their physical being, the Giza pyramids were more symbolic.

The sheer scale of these gigantic tombs and the massive construction problems they must have faced still amazes visitors today — but the real enigma of the pyramids is the accuracy of the geometry. The tolerances involved are incredible when you think that the base of Kephren's, (big enough to swallow six football pitches) is a perfect square to within 15 millimetres! But it wasn't just their fantastic construction accuracy that was important, it was also the relationship of the size to their lives. The base of Khufu's pyramid shows a relationship to the length of the sun-year; using Egyptian measurements it has been determined that the circumference corresponds to the sun-year to within two decimal places.

Exacting geometry, astronomical relationships, and the obsession with death, give the architecture of Ancient Egypt mystical qualities that has fascinated and will continue to fascinate man forever. The symbolism architecture can convey was first seen in Egypt, and later used by the great Mediterranean Empires.

WEST ASIATIC

Within West Asiatic architecture there are three main recognizable periods: Babylonian, Assyrian, and Persian. All these cultures developed within the fertile plains between two rivers, the Tigris and Euphrates. Due to the very nature of the region, stone and timber suitable for building use, were scarce commodities, but there was an abundance of clay to use as the basic blocks for construction. Similar to the Egyptians, the facing of the walls and the decorations put upon them were fundamental to the style. Both the Babylonians and the Assyrians used rough block work as the core material, dressed together with slabs of glowing alabaster and glazed brickwork of many colors.

As in Egypt, the building construction was determined by the availability of the raw materials at hand. Whereas the Nile Valley supplied sufficient stone of a size to span wide openings and large columns, Western Asia had to use smaller units — thus they devised corbeled horizontal courses to form arches. Because large stones were not employed, unfortunately we have very little evidence as to the imposing beauty of the structures of this time — the stepped ziggurats, towering palaces, and great staircases and ramps sweeping up to vast platforms. Persia, unlike Babylon and Assyria, had resources of stone to create columns and was able to take some architectural elements from Egypt and Asiatic Greece, as well as inheriting forms from Assyrian architecture. Again they made great use of decoration — not only for the aesthetics but also for religious symbolism.

The stone remnants that can be found across the Western Asiatic region show tell-tale signs that the origins of their construction techniques stemmed from the use of wood. All the techniques found in timber construction can be seen in the remains: elements such as notched beams, tightening wedges and rafter ends. The influence of timber on construction was not only confined to the Middle East; the practice is evident in Greek architecture — for example, the Bactrian Greeks in India reproduced timber forms in stone. Timber may have been the original material in general use for primitive buildings, but it gave way to the durable stone, and the nature of this material eventually governed architectural character.

Beyond the site of the Parthenon is its predecessor, the little temple of Erechtheum, which played a bigger part in the rituals of the goddess Athene.

GREEK ARCHITECTURE

Whether or not you take the opinion that Greek architecture is beyond criticism and a standard by which all successive periods of architecture may be tested, what is not in dispute is the influence the ancient societies of Greece have had on the western world. For most of its history Greece has not been a single country but a number of city-states, usually in conflict, scattered over the mainland and the surrounding islands. In the

Hellenic period Athens exerted its supremacy over the region. From this arose the high classical age; the flowering of architecture, art, literature, philosophy and drama. Among the achievements of this age was the construction of the Parthenon.

The most sacred of ancient Greece's sacred sites, Delphi was the sanctuary of Apollo and the source of the oracle.

In general, it is the philosophical structures behind architecture that leads commentators to speak in terms of "timelessness" when describing the impact of a style. The philosophy behind Greek architecture was to discover the eternally valid rules that dictate form and proportion; to construct buildings of human scale that were suited to the divinity of their gods; Classical Greek architecture is "ideal architecture." The fact that elements of the style have been copied for over 2,500 years means that their intentions of validation were justified. The jewel in the crown of Classical Greek architecture still remains the Parthenon which many see as the near perfect building, this illustrates the importance the Greeks placed on their religious and civic structures. However, whereas Greek temples and public buildings were of the very greatest splendor, their private residences were simple single-storey constructions, built from cheap materials.

From the invading Persians, the Greeks learned the principles of constructing arches, and luckily the materials they required to build temples — stone and marble — were readily available all around them. However, as with the Egyptians, Greek architecture was trabeated rather than arcuated — based on the beam and the flat roof rather than the arch — and their architectural heritage came from the wooden construction techniques, which they showed great respect for. The Greek architects learnt much from other Mediterranean civilizations — principally the plan from West Asiatic, and the columnar form from Egypt.

The bold simplicity of the Doric temple form — typically Greek in evolution — used unity of design and decoration to emphasize the structure. The Heraion at Olympia is the earliest Doric temple to survive; its original wooden columns having been replaced at a later date by stone. In all of the existing early examples of Doric temples, the columns are stocky and primitive. Through time, refinements were made, culminating in the Parthenon (447–438 BC) with its seemingly perfect proportions and well-balanced relationship between sculptural art and architecture. In the desire for the utopian splendor, measures were taken to overcome the optical illusion of concavity by employing a slight convex curve to the columns. A progression from the simple, to the more exquisite, is revealed in the temple of Athena Nike (448–421 BC) and the Erechtheum (421–406 BC), whose tendencies were toward a new appreciation of architectural movement. It wasn't long before the role of the architect became secondary to that of the sculptor as the desire for richer ornamentation grew — as exemplified in the Mausoleum of Halicarnassus (350–330 BC). Greek architectural development reached a peak when the Coragic Monument of Lysicrates, Athens (335-334 BC) illustrated an overworked elegance, leading to its great popularity.

It wasn't just temples where the Greeks excelled; theatres such as that of Dionysus, sited under the Acropolis, (arguably the grandest of its type) displayed an enormous understanding of acoustics that even rivaled their aesthetic sensibilities.

If Greek architecture was the birth of classical architecture, then surely its abiding bequest to architecture as a whole — the element that instantly conjures up elegance and a sense of quality — is found in the Greek Orders; Doric, Ionic and later Corinthian. These conventional systems of beams and columns were developed for temple colonnades, but were since modified to be used in a wider context. Although not always strictly functional, their flexibility and expressive forms have ensured lasting popularity.

ROMAN ARCHITECTURE

Architecture was inextricably entwined with the art of the Roman Empire. Above all else to the Romans, architecture was social art, meant as a benefit to the community. Outwardly Roman architecture owes much to the influences of Greek architecture; however, it was through Rome that many elements were made popular. The architecture the Greeks practiced, a series of logical steps to achieve a balance between the horizontals and the verticals — "sublimated carpentry" — is quite different from the rounded forms of arches, vaults and domes that epitomized Ancient Rome, and which gave the structures a more "plastic" or molded feel. Whereas the Greeks held the column as the important focus of the architecture, the Romans often relegated it to mere decoration, giving emphasis to the wall, evident in temples such the Maison Carrée, Nimes (c.19 BC). The focus was given to the Corinthian order, elaborately carved entablatures and other ornamentation. The great domes and vaults of the Romans were constructed from concrete and brick, their surfaces stuccoed or clad in marble. The earliest examples of concrete used in domes is that of the Stabian Baths, Pompeii, while the earliest large-scale vault was that of the Tabalarium in Rome. It was here that the first important instance of decoration and function separating occurred, where half-columns were used ornamentally. Concrete had also been used for the construction of barrel vaults such as those in Nero's Golden House, the Baths of Caracalla and the Basilica Nova of Maxentius.

Built by the Emperors Vespasian, Titus and Domitian, the Colosseum in Rome shows a complexity in design, which had to be worked out mathematically.

The Pantheon in Rome (c. AD 100–125) is the pinnacle of Roman architecture. It stands as a lasting testament to the engineering prowess of the Romans, because the sheer simplicity of the composition clearly defines it as a masterpiece. Based on a sphere, the height of the walls is equal to the radius of the dome. Comparison between the Parthenon and the Pantheon, shows the contrast between the Greeks and the Romans; the former being of an extrovert nature, whereas the latter being much more introverted — something that can also be seen in the Basilica, a large meeting hall used in public administration.

In domestic architecture three types were developed: the *domus* or town house; the *insula* or multi-story apartment house; and the *villa* or suburban or country house.

The domus took its name from the Greek house and was usually single-storied and inward looking; an atrium was at the center of a symmetrically axial plan. The façade presented to the street was often plain with no windows, and sometimes let for shop use. The insula had identical but separate floors in a vaulted concrete construction. In Rome their height was limited to 75 feet to conform to the decree past by Emperor Augustus. The great fire of Rome in AD 64 meant that rebuilt new quarters were laid out symmetrically along arcaded streets and set around public squares. More casual and straggling than the domus, the villa derived from the traditional farmhouse. It, too, was more outward looking and had great variety of planning and room shapes, especially in the luxurious examples. Porticoes and colonnades enlivened the exteriors, and due to the surroundings, light and shade played key roles in design decisions.

Today the Byzantine Hagia Sophia in Istanbul is covered in the patterns of Islam: geometrical and calligraphic forms, and with cylindrical minarets at the corners that give the mosques such distinctive silhouettes.

Imperial Roman architecture at its best can be seen in Hadrian's villa at Tivoli (c. AD 123) and the Diocletian's Palace in Split (c. AD 300), the latter representing the last great architectural monument of the Roman Empire prior to the disintegration of the Pax Romana. Here, too, the experimentation that the Romans frequently displayed is evident in the decorative elements, a language later seen in Byzantine architecture. The language present in the basilicas closed the divide architecturally between the Western Roman Empire and the Eastern Empire of Byzantium, (linked by early Christianity) that became an important architectural inspiration in the coming ten centuries. Before the death of Constantine in AD 337, work had begun on the church of St. Peter in Rome and he had transferred the imperial capital to Byzantium, in the process renaming it Constantinople (now Istanbul).

EARLY CHRISTIAN AND BYZANTINE

It wasn't until after AD 200 that Christian structures started to appear, primarily in three forms — meeting houses, catacombs and martyria. The meeting rooms contained an assembly room for the Eucharist celebrations, a baptistery and various other rooms. The Christian Basilica evolved from the fact that Constantine recognized Christianity in AD 313, and churches superseded the modest meeting houses whose models were Roman administrative halls, not the pagan temples of the time. At first the architecture of the Constantinian church varied from the aisleless halls to centralized buildings, though the latter were usually martyria. Heathen cults were banned in 39, thus promoting Christianity as the official religion of the Roman Empire, and the basilica attained its canonical form such as that at San Maria Maggiore, Rome (432–40 AD).

The culmination of early Christian architecture came in the form of Byzantine architecture, a style developed after AD 330 in Byzantium on the Bosphorus. Constantine, having moved the imperial capital of the Empire, spared no effort in recreating a traditionally Roman city, but instead a gradual transition into a new style emerged.

Many changes occurred to alter the interpretation of the original classical thinking — perhaps the most fundamental being that the orders so important to both the Greeks and Romans were ignored. Flat lacy ornaments replaced the relief decorations that were so popular in Rome alongside a general coarsening of the classical details. Early churches in Cilicia showed clear indications that the influences were not only from the West but also from the East. Despite signs that there was a departure from classical precepts, Byzantine art and architecture shows a desire to recapture the splendors of the classical past. The forms of church, which had evolved in this time, were the martyria and the basilica, the former being built on a Greek cross plan and domed; a combination of a dome with a square base being a Byzantine introduction from the near East. The most striking feature of the Byzantine church was the wholly unclassical play of void and solid, dark and light, in the interiors that arose from the combining of the two forms to create an effect of mystery. A perfect example of this is Hagia Sophia, in today's Istanbul (AD 532–37) which to this day is still the outstanding masterpiece, it was not so much the emotive, but rather the intellectual and mathematical qualities that impressed contemporaries. At this point mathematics was considered the highest of all the sciences, and Hagia Sophia's architect, Anthemios, believed that architecture was "the application of geometry to solid matter."

A complex triple symbolism began to play a greater part in Byzantine church architecture, as the church became regarded as a microcosm of the earth and the sky, as the setting of Christ's life on earth and, at the same time, as the image of the liturgical year. This symbolism was expressed in mosaic or painted decoration: the very colors used had an emblematic significance, as did the mystique of numbers. Equally as important as the air of mystery created by screens and galleries dividing the well-lit central area from those surrounding it, were the intellectual concepts. The perfect background to display elaborate decoration was in the typical Byzantine church plan or cross-in-square, a Greek cross inscribed in a square and capped with a dome and subsidiary domes. But a crisis developed in Byzantium from the seventh century and continuing into the ninth: the protracted and enigmatic Iconoclast controversy whose resolution in favor of the holy images made comprehensive alterations to East Christian architecture. The Middle Byzantine decorative system had predicted appropriate forms of which the cross-in-square church developed as the characteristic type.

Massive stone towers are all that remains of the 11th century Sas-Bahu Temple in Udaipur, India.

It wasn't long before the influence of Byzantine architecture made its presence felt in Italy, although Western peculiarities revealed themselves especially in the external decorations: for example, San Marco, Venice has a rich marble-clad exterior.

The cross-in-square church type proliferated in throughout the middle and late Byzantine periods, in Russia it outlived the Fall of Constantinople (1453) by at least two centuries Greater attention to the exterior surfaces coincided with the its increased spread to surrounding areas, leading almost inevitably to the fussy later examples.

ARCHITECTURE OF THE EAST

The traditional architecture of South and East Asia has been profoundly influenced by the spread from India of Buddhism and Hinduism. In particular, the religious philosophies of the region are vividly expressed in the decoration of the buildings. Chronologically, Eastern development does not parallel the Western story; instead of a series of styles and trends, the architecture of Eastern civilizations remained static for many centuries, much as that of the Ancient Egyptians. As with so many early civilizations, the primary material used for building was local wood, but soon stone was used after it was accepted as a "sacred" material. As in the early Western architecture, techniques learned from wood construction were extensively employed when stone was first used.

Shallow walled arcading finished in bands of red and white marble make up the exteriors of Pisa's Cathedral, Baptistery and Campanile.

Early Hindu temples consisted of rooms carved from solid rock faces; they were supplanted by freestanding structures that were built in southern India from about the eighth century AD. These reflected individual daily devotion to public ritual. Distributed over the subcontinent, Hindu temples survive in great numbers, revealing rich carved figurative decorations, displaying sensuous and erotic characters. Styles are not in periods — but rather according to the districts, the three main styles being Chalukyan, Northern and Dravidian.

Buddhism is strongly community-oriented, leading to the establishment of monasteries, *viharas*, with cells grouped round courtyards, *chaitya* or assembly halls, and *stupas*. The concept of the world in the middle of a great universe is the underlying force in Buddhism and Hinduism. The center of the world is a great mountain made of ascending terraces. Mankind occupies the bottom terrace; guardian deities live on the middle tiers and at the top are the 27 heavens of the gods. A vast number of architectural forms and details can be traced back to this basic concept, and mirrored in the ziggurats and pyramids of the West.

Due to the insular nature of the people within the region of the Asian sub-continent and their strong philosophical religions, there was no need for the usual Western diversity of styles. The East developed a style that fitted their divine requirements and they felt no need to diverge from this path. Their influence on the world of architecture, after the initial skin-deep treatment of applied decoration, is now visible in styles of the West like Minimalism, Eastern theories of religious enlightenment, and Zen qualities.

ROMANESQUE

Romanesque architecture was the first real Western European style, and the first that provided a stylistic unity; indeed, as far as central Europe is concerned, it would seem as if all the builders and craftsmen had been pupils of one and the same master. This unity is due in most part to the unity of religion — particularly the monastic centers. These had developed from settlements founded by missionaries since the fifth century

AD. At first they were farming communities on land that had been cleared around the local church, then monasteries soon came to be built according to an approved plan, of which the most significant examples were Riechenau and St. Gall. Monasteries were first realized in the East in conjunction with monks' cells; deriving from the Greek word meaning "alone," they were places where monks gathered for communal meditation and communal living.

As early as AD 530 Nursia had laid down explicit rules for the monastic life when he founded Monte Cassino in central Italy: regular divine service, communal meals and communal dormitories. The acceptance of the Benedictine Rule as a model by the Frankish Emperor Charlemagne, and continued by Louis the Pious after him, saw the start of Carolingian architecture. The addition of monastery schools solidified the Benedictine conception from which later monastic orders were derived. Stylistic unity followed the cohesion of these widely different rules in spite of continual political confusion; Christian power was the superior building patron in the Dark Ages.

The word "Romanesque" only came to be widely used in the 19th century, before then other names had been used to describe the early medieval period. Byzantine was used as long as there remained an obvious connection to Constantinople. Other names such as neo-Greek or old-German do not truthfully represent the style, as there is no particular region that dominated its development. Romanesque is appropriate as it recalls the origin of the stylistic features: the basilica, the round Roman arch and the arcaded courtyard. All building that were erected between the end of the 10th century and the beginning of the 13th could have the term applied to them.

To begin with the Romanesque architects continued to use and develop the Carolingian vernacular. As in previous periods the works were predominately ecclesiastical in nature, and through accentuation of the western façade, the basilica received a new face. Towers now started to emerge to flank the western entrance, often extending beyond the breadth of the building: and so the west front was created. The demons of darkness supposedly came out of the western sunset, and so a common trait emerged of naming the towers after the archangels, echoing heathen beliefs. A significant difference from the old basilica is the increased emphasis on the crossing, the space that the nave shares with the transepts as they cross at right angles; the nave is extended eastwards because of this space. From this arises the choir that forms a single spatial unit with the apse widened to the width of the nave. The double-chanceled church, (a characteristic of German Romanesque as in Worms Cathedral) has a choir at each end of the nave.

Grotesque figures, human or animal in form, were a startling component of medieval architecture. As well as being water spouts, they were used as decorative tools.

Early Romanesque architecture shows little use of domes or barrel vaults; the nave was usually surmounted by a ceiling which was secured to the rafters of the saddle roof. Barrel vaults covering both the nave and transepts to create a cross did not come to prominence until after the year 1100. As well the cruciform vault, another method was often employed to close the space above the nave and transepts; separate higher vaulting with either a barrel or a dome from which the later cross-ribbed vault evolved. The spread of the rib vault and the pointed vault, however, is usually a sign of the approaching Gothic style.

MEDIEVAL AND GOTHIC

It is not often that the start of a style can be accurately pinpointed, but in the case of the transition between Romanesque and Gothic such a watershed exists. In 1144 a Benedictine abbot called Suger embarked on the rebuilding of St. Denis in Paris after a fire. Before he did so, he set out in writing his aims and thoughts for the presence of the new abbey. The abbot's book gives many indications to symbolic references; numbers become significant, and intentions are named and given reasons.

Salisbury, the classic English cathedral, was built on a virgin site to a uniform plan.

> *"The nave is supported by 12 columns, corresponding to the 12 apostles, with just as many in the aisles, corresponding to the 12 prophets. Thus fulfilled the words of the apostles who built in the spirit: So you are no longer guests and strangers, but fellow-citizens with the saints and members of God's house, which is built upon the foundation of the apostles and the prophets, with Jesus as the cornerstone unifying both walls, and in which every building, be it spiritual or material, grows to become a holy temple in the Lord."*

Gothic architecture saw the creation of soaring arches, to draw the spirit of man up to heaven, and transformed walls into screens of glass which would teach the worshipper the origins of the faith in pictures, (for a largely illiterate congregation) as well as submerging him in celestial light. In Gothic church architecture, all things should be ordered toward God, the worshipper's eyes drawn first to God-made-man in the sacrament of the altar at the east end of the church, then upward to God-in-heaven.

Originally known as "*le style ogival*," it was called "Gothic" or "barbaric" in the 16th century by the art historian Giorgio Vasari. The power of St. Denis had an immediate effect. Within 25 years of its consecration, every diocese represented at the ceremony had raised a Gothic cathedral of its own.

None of the features by which we distinguish the style today was new; all the elements had been used before. What the Gothic designers had done was combine the elements in new ways. First, unlike the Romanesque arch, the pointed arch gave a freedom to the width of the structure while remaining the same height. This made possible arcades where some columns were closer than others, but with all the tops of the arches the same height. The use of the pointed arch opened up further possibilities in the structure, allowing the main forces of the roof to be transposed to the ground via flying buttresses, thus rendering the walls as panels which could be constructed almost entirely from glass.

The decorative elements of Gothic architecture became highly developed in buildings of the English Decorated style (13th–14th century) and the French Flamboyant style (15th–16th century). These styles are exemplified by the tower of Salisbury Cathedral and the staircase in the church of St. Maclou. In both buildings, embellishments such as ballflowers and curvilinear tracery were used liberally. The English Perpendicular style (late 14th–15th century) emphasized the vertical and horizontal elements of a building, tectonic in nature similar to that of the ancient Greeks. Key to the decoration were the windows, since the paring down of the solid wall meant that glass took over. From the early simple lancets — as at Coutances (1220–91) — to the plate tracery of Chartres (1194–1221) through to bar tracery as in Wells Cathedral (1215–39), the skills of the masons gave the windows prominence. These skills had grown over the years, promoted through association with the East and the free trade of masons' labor across the continent, something that also led to the interchange of ideas and techniques.

The emphasis on verticality is reaches its peak in countries such as Germany and Bohemia, whose architects liked to express this by towers and ascending spires — for example those of Ulm Minster. But the initial impetus in the development of the pillars came from France and England. A particularly rich period in England came in the first half of the 14th century, during which time emerged window, vaulting and roofing styles that were highly influential in the rest of Europe.

Gothic architecture had its effect on secular buildings as well; its influence was seen in the later 14th century, particularly in the building of castles. These castles retained the weighty fortifications of old, but saw an increase in decorative features, a change that would accelerate during the Renaissance. As well as the church and the nobles, the increase in world trade saw wealthy merchants in a position to construct houses in the Gothic style. These houses were seen as proof of the merchants' social standing, reflecting their wealth and importance. An extreme example of this wealth can be seen in that ultimate trading center, Venice, whose Doges' Palace (1309–1424) shows characteristic splendor, simple massing with a delicate double row of arcades and patterned marble upper story.

Unsurprisingly, national forms of Gothic were manifested in exhibitions of local civic pride in structures such as local town halls. At the forefront were those in Germany and the Low Countries whose burghers expressed their commercial and social pride in steeped pitched roofs and decorative towers. But they didn't always get it right. Often their attempts led to clumsy and undignified results; the balance required in the massing to truly show the qualities of the Gothic style was seldom reproduced to great effect in the secular use. The Palazzo Vecchio in Florence illustrates this awkwardness in achieving the balance, and it is in Florence where the transition to Renaissance architecture started.

Using Brunelleschi's dome in Florence as a model, Michelangelo designed a double shell and rib dome surmounted by a lantern, in keeping with the intentions of his predecessor, Bramante.

RENAISSANCE

At the same time as Milan Cathedral, (arguably the greatest and only true Gothic cathedral in Italy) was under construction, Brunelleschi was designing a domed cathedral for Florence that would spark the next major movement within architecture. There was nothing new in domes, but the difference was that Brunelleschi invented a complicated wooden form allowing his eight-paneled dome to rest on top of an octagonal drum. This drum, constructed of an inner and an outer masonry shell, also used masonry ribs tied together in a series of reinforcing chains made of bands of timber or stone, clamped with iron. To prevent the dome from spreading apart, the cupola on top acted as a weight to hold everything together.

Standing on a stepped podium above the entrance to the Grand Canal, the church is an octagon with a high drum crowned by a large dome.

Another influential building by Brunelleschi was the Foundling Hospital of 1421, a simple and serene structure with slim graceful Corinthian columns and plain rectangular windows directly above. However, the quintessential early Renaissance building was the chapel created for the Pazzi family's Franciscan friary of Santa Croce (1429–61).

The Pazzi Chapel used a revolutionary form — a cube covered by a dome — as opposed to the now-traditional nave and aisles shape, and placed the center of the chapel at the centre of the circle below the dome. Great care was taken to create a structure that seemed to be complete from any direction, with close attention to the treatment of wall surfaces clearly indicating the proportions. Two of Brunelleschi's great churches, San Lorenzo (1421) and Santo Spirito (1436–82), had basilican plans, but the same exactitude was there and domes were used at the crossings. This new style, known today as Renaissance, would dominate architecture for centuries: first in Europe, then spreading across much of the developed world. It can still be seen in today's buildings.

The Renaissance acquired its name from the Italian words *rinascimento* or *rinascita* meaning rebirth. These words were widely used by contemporary writers to discuss the restoration of ancient Roman standards and motifs. Today we understand the term to mean primarily Italian art and architecture from, roughly, 1420 to the mid-16th century. In countries other than Italy the Renaissance started by the adoption of Italian motifs, but the subsequent styles had less in common with the qualities of the Italian Renaissance — the detail of ancient Roman derivation and a sense of stability and poise.

The cause of the transition from Gothic to Renaissance was in part simply because Gothic had had its day, but it was also because of the influx of exiles from Constantinople during its years of war against the Turk that culminated in the fall of the city in 1453. The exiles brought with them books containing knowledge long forgotten in the West. Art and literature received fresh impetus; the rebirth of the old was celebrated, and Hellenistic architectural forms began to supplant everything Gothic.

The impact of this revival sparked the imaginations of architectural theorists: Alberti, Serlio, Francesco di Giorgio, Palladio, Vignola, Giulio Romano. Architecture was no longer just the continuation of a practical tradition, it became a literary idea; the architect was seen as a theorist, not just a builder. The rediscovery of one of Pythagoras's theories — that musical intervals in harmony were exactly proportional to numbers in physical dimensions — gave architects a basis for proportions, linking music and architecture via mathematics. Here was an example of nature displaying a sense of unity, and so it followed that a building could reflect the fundamental laws of nature and God in its dimensions.

Leon Battista Alberti brought these theories together. Using Euclidean geometry and the harmony of numbers, Alberti worked out the ideal proportions from these figures. One of the crucial Renaissance definitions of beauty in a structure is the rational integration of the proportions of all the parts, where nothing could be added or subtracted without destroying the harmony of the whole. The individual is also a crucial aspect of Alberti's theories. He elevated man from the medieval idea of "created in God's image and likeness" to the adage of the ancient Greek philosopher Protagoras, that "man is the measure of all things." It is this that led Alberti to superimpose the human figure on a centralized cruciform church plan, thus indicating that buildings should reflect the proportions of the human figure. All of Alberti's buildings were carefully proportioned, and created many of the characteristic details that would later appear in hundreds of Renaissance buildings.

Though started in Florence, the new style quickly spread to other great cities of Italy, first Rome, then on to Venice. Encouraged by papal patronage, the phase from 1500 onwards is known as the High Renaissance, dominated in the early years by Donato Bramante. He built on what was then thought to be the site of St. Peter's martyrdom, Tempietto, San Pietro in Monotrio, Rome. Although very modest, Tempietto has been used as a template for structures around the world including St. Paul's in London, the Capitol Building in Washington D.C. and the most recognized example of Renaissance architecture in Rome, St. Peter's. Built on the old basilica that dated back to AD 330, the foundation stone was laid in 1506; it would take until 1626 to complete, and the list of contributing architects reads like a who's who of the period; Bramante, Raphael, Peruzzi, Sangallo the Younger, Michelangelo, Vignola, della Porta, Fontana and Carlo Maderna.

The Renaissance would have an abiding effect on later architects. Here one can see the Renaissance at work in Vanbrugh's Castle Howard, dating from the early years of the 18th century

Michelangelo designed the dome of St. Peter's, inspired by Brunelleschi's dome in Florence. Michelangelo, who turned to architecture in his later years, left significant hallmarks that many after him used. One such was the seeming disregard for size in Renaissance architecture, opening up new concepts of scale and space, areas with which Baroque would later experiment. Palladio adopted another Michelangelo trait with his use of giant orders, columns running up through two or more stories.

The Renaissance's third center was Venice, and its leading figure Andrea Palladio, a precise and exact classicist. Villa Capra (Rotunda) near Vicenza (1565–69) displays both controlled classical and Alberti's rules. Palladio's work in Vicenza reflects the new importance of secular rather than religious buildings. But it's the sheer elegance of Palladio's buildings that had a profound influence on later architects — particularly the Georgians in 18th century England and others as far afield as Russia and the United States. Palladio effortlessly achieves a humanity in his buildings while at the same time exhibiting exactitude and a centralized plan, often qualities lacking in formal classical buildings. The Renaissance began to spread across Europe at the same time that it began to decline in Italy. By the beginning of the 16th century it had reached France. Much of Europe was still producing Gothic architecture, so not all the European countries adopted Renaissance styles in their original clarity of form. Appearing frequently in moderation and with a distinct avoidance of the obvious Italianate element, the Renaissance style would become the choice of international merchants' houses, mercantile depots and multi-storied gables of town halls.

Characterized by its exuberant decoration, a sense of mass and expansive curvaceous forms, the Baroque style applies fully only in Italy, Germany, Austria and Spain.

The declining period of the Renaissance is known as "Mannerism," which is derived from the French *manier* signifying style. Intended to imply a high personal method of expression and the adoption of one master's personal style by another, it does not justify its conception. Instigated by Michelangelo, it tended toward exaggeration, tricks of perspective and theatrical effects.

The coming and going of artists was not the only way ideas permeated through Europe; pattern books started to emerge from Italy, and many architects who hadn't seen ancient ruins relied heavily on these books. Out of this, some exceptional architects, such as Philibert de l'Orme, created extraordinary elements by picking out ideas and pairing them with others. However, many of the Classical motifs were misapplied out of context, with no reference to the past, and the Renaissance effect was only skin deep. To compound it all, a drawback of learning from books is in the very nature of two-dimensional images. Many architects of the time failed to grasp the importance of the three-dimensional nature of architecture, and consequently much of the work retains the qualities found in the books.

Here, too, as in Italy there began a shift to secular buildings, partly because the vast number of Gothic churches rendered redundant the need for new structures. In bourgeois Europe, where prosperous housing was emerging, architects were in demand for smaller commissions. It was during this time that England started a campaign of building houses for rich merchants; they modified Tudor and Jacobean plans and began to rely on their own needs instead of Gothic and Italian Renaissance influences.

Distinctive types emerged throughout Europe. For example, in England the houses were striped vertically down their wide frontages with slightly projecting bay windows, and emphasized horizontally with thin string courses separating the ranks of mullioned windows. However, Palladio's influence still remained strong, particularly in Holland, where compact palaces expressing all the virtues of elegance and dignity were produced. These palaces, though fitting a domestic scale, fulfilled Alberti's desire for the perfect proportions; parts so integrated that nothing can be added or taken away without destroying the harmony of the whole.

This same quality is clearly apparent in the work of Inigo Jones in England, who visited many Palladian buildings and carefully studied Palladio's work. Palladian unity was a paramount concern to Jones, "The outward ornaments ought to be solid, proportional according to the rules, masculine and unaffected." Jones created the first English villa in the Italian style with the Queen's House at Greenwich (1616–35), a series of cubes connected by bridges. But it was his work with John Webb on the reconstruction of Wilton House, Wiltshire, in 1647 that escalated a diversity and wealth of inspiration in Renaissance architecture into more spectacular movements that would come to prominence in the 17th century — Baroque and Rococo.

BAROQUE AND ROCOCO

A pearl which is not perfectly round is called *barocco* in Portuguese and Italian, *barock* in German, and *baroque* in French. In time, baroque came to mean bizarre. In the 19th century Baroque became the acknowledged description for the style that superseded the Renaissance in about 1600. Used at first only to describe an architectural type, it quickly went on to describe a distinct style in all the arts, a style that expressed itself with rejoiced in the use of the curved line with exuberantly sweeping gestures and rounded human figures to the point of being grandiloquent.

The Baroque is commonly listed as happening between 1600 and 1760, but there was no specific starting point — as with many styles it came about through a series of evolutionary stages. Growing from Renaissance's Mannerism period, Baroque took these fundamental forms and began to strive toward a new harmony that allowed one to overflow into the other, disguising their constructive textures and thus confusing the limits of the arts. Architecture, sculpture and painting are no longer entities that are treated separately but are inextricably intertwined to create three-dimensional visions of heaven and cloudscapes of allegorical events. This interaction characterized the Baroque style, one where exuberance, ostentation and boisterous profusion are celebrated.

Arguably Gibbs's finest work, the Radcliffe Camera in simple terms is the drum and domes of a cathedral, most of which were influenced by Bramante's Tempietto.

St. Peter's of Rome is a clear example of how the Baroque style grew from Renaissance beginnings. First conceived in 1450 to occupy where the old basilica had once stood, successive popes and architects all added their contribution over the next 200 years. The major influences were Bramante's initial Greek cross plan (1506) that was later revised by Michelangelo (1547); then later still, Carlo Maderna, (considered a Baroque artist) presided over the project for 22 years until its consecration in 1626. In 1646 Lorenzo Bernini attempted to construct the western towers but, due to foundation problems this was abandoned; he later went on to work on the interior and created the colonnaded piazza. Like Michelangelo before him, he was first a sculptor then an architect. Andreas Schluter, who again was primarily a sculptor, undertook further ornamentation to the exterior façade.

The Baroque is the style of Catholic countries; it typifies the rejuvenation, which flowered as a result of the Counter-Reformation. The transition to secular buildings did not prove successful as the colossal expenditure involved made the style a symbol of worldly absolutism; the art of great princes. In its last period, known as Rococo, the style became reduced in scale, moving toward lighter, more frivolous, variants. The bourgeoisie could now adopt the style with fewer misgivings.

The Woods of Bath created a unified vision of town planning that has since been copied throughout Great Britain.

Rococo, from the French word *rocaille* meaning shell work, was eminently suited to interior decoration; it featured constantly recurring decorative motifs both in the painting and in the stucco work. The building principles of Baroque were taken across into Rococo but on a reduced scale; the oval ground plan is found more frequently as is the corresponding basket-arch. Both of these elements give a lighter effect to the finished building. Everything is curved in this style, more as a form of decoration than out of any technical necessity; cupolas are often only there for the sake of appearances.

Just as the early Renaissance was Italian, the Rococo was French. But in France the word is rarely used. The French prefer to divide the age of elegance into three periods: Regence, Louis Quinze and Louis Seize, the later showing the transition to neo-Classicism. The new decoration is often asymmetrical and abstract, naturalistic flowers, trees, whole rustic scenes, and also Chinese motifs are sometimes playfully introduced into Rococo.

In French external architecture the Rococo is only noticeable by a greater elegance and delicacy, quite the opposite from German and Austrian Rococo which influenced the exterior considerably more. Delicately curved façades sparring in architectural detail apart from fine ornamental stucco-work. The best examples are the small palaces in the Nymphenburg Park in Munich and Sans Souci at Potsdam.

ROMANTIC CLASSICISM AND NEO-CLASSICISM

Coming to an abrupt end in the 18th century, Baroque and Rococo gave way to a more sober architecture, reflective of the ponderous political empires that were now exerting their power. This change was brought about not only by the political upheavals in the European powers, but Baroque had only been taken up in certain countries like France and Protestant Germany. There was a desire for a newfound expression in the fashionable taste of the time. There was a need in the turbulent times for an architecture that showed permanence and stability, a far cry from the gaiety of Baroque and Rococo.

First expressed in England and Scotland, architects made a return to classicism not of the Greek or Roman origin, but the interpretations by Andreas Palladio. Colen Campbell, a young Scot, produced a book of over 100 engravings of houses in Britain, *Vitruvius Britannicus*, in which he praised both Palladio and Indigo Jones. His theories were put into practice when he built Houghton Hall and then a villa in Kent, Mereworth (1723), which was a reinterpretation of Villa Carpa. Lord Burlington built a similar villa on the outskirts of London, Chiswick House (1725), with the help of William Kent.

It was Lord Burlington, a Whig politician and an amateur architect, who brought together a group of architects who used Palladio as a role model. With the likes of Colen Campbell and William Kent, the Palladian style was carried as far as Pushkin in Russia, with Charles Cameron adding a wing to the imperial palace at Tsarskoe Selo (1787). Even architects who were trained in the Baroque, such as James Gibbs, produced works like St. Martin-in-the-Fields (1721–26) and Senate House, Cambridge (1722–30) that revealed Palladian elements with a dignified symmetry. This simple sophistication of the Palladian way of building was not only used for country houses and civic buildings, but through John Wood the elder and John Wood the younger; they translated the style to create streets. The Royal Crescent, Bath (1767–75), although a terrace, reflects all the elegance and drama of a Palladian villa, and thus altered the perception of town planning.

The Burlington School pioneered the association of architecture and landscape, through William Kent in particular. This new awareness reversed the Baroque relation of the inside and outside that was seen in France. The simple clean interiors of the Palladian style contrasted with free-flowing landscapes. The most celebrated of the new gardeners was Capability Brown, whose work lead to the Picturesque movement, where the garden became an outside room filled with delightful architectural features and follies. This new relationship was strengthened by Abbé Laugier in his *Essai sur l'architecture* of 1753, in which he contended the ideal architecture. The first translation of this theory into practice was Jaques Germain Soufflot's Ste-Geneviève, later renamed the Panthéon, Paris (1755–92); however, due to the politics of the times, his full intentions were foiled. Further weight was added when Lord Shaftesbury persuaded James Stuart and Nicholas Revett to visit Athens in the 1750s, culminating in their work *The Antiques of Athens*.

As with the Renaissance, there was soon support in the form of books, treatises, sketches, paintings and engravings, which all played a part in the demise of the Baroque. Toward the second half of the 18th century a stricter and more scholarly style came to the forefront, neo-Classicism, the dominant figure of which was Robert Adam. After taking the Grand Tour, visiting the ancient sites of Rome and Athens, Adam interpreted the classical order and motifs to reinvent Etruscan decoration. There was scarcely a house designed by Adam that did not contain an Etruscan room. But not content with creating the spaces, Adam would be involved in the furniture and all internal details. He gave equal attention to his other rooms including a Roman room. His remodeled Syon House in west London (1762–69) actually incorporated old Roman columns dredged from the River Tiber.

The Capitol in Washington D.C., though having a basic Parthenon shape, is truly fixed in the 19th century with its cast-iron dome.

The spread of neo-Classicism within Britain was not limited to London and the Home Counties: examples could be seen as far as Edinburgh and Glasgow. A great number of the major towns and cities in Great Britain had their character changed. It was in this period of continual revival of past styles that many architects made their name, creating what we regard today as traditional; among the luminaries were Nash, Wyatt and Walpole.

Revivalism wasn't purely the preserve of the British; the movement had crossed the sea to the Continent and flourished in isolated pockets with mixed results. Unlike the royal architect Agne-Jacques Gabriel, who retained his classical symmetry and composure, Richard Mique was influenced by English romanticism, seen in his Le Petit Trianon, Versailles (1778). More prominent were Claude-Nicolas Ledoux and Etiene Louis Boullée who displayed architecture of fantastic grandeur; La Barrière de la Villette being one of Ledoux's best surviving tollhouses of Paris.

The Gothic Revival clock tower of Westminster Palace,commonly known as Big Ben, although that is correctly the name of the bell inside.

The extreme end of neo-Classicism in Europe can be found in Germany, famously by Karl Friedrich Schinkel who straddled several styles and eras, but also showed a romantic side, having studied under firstly Friedrich Gilly, then Ledoux and Boullée in Paris. Schinkel's best known buildings, the Schauspielhaus (1819–21) and the Altes Museum (1823–30) in Berlin are both in the Greek idiom.

COLONIAL

From the Americas to the Far East and Australia, the colonies of the great powers of Europe were influenced by the architectural movements in Europe.It wasn't, however, a one-way street: the colonizers pushed the architectural styles they knew — with the adaptations necessitated by local conditions, availability of materials and the skills of local craftsman — but were in turn influenced by the buildings they saw in their colonies. These factors produced variations of styles that had a hallmark unique to the region and often had an effect on the architecture within the colonizing country.

In the early days of colonization — particularly of the Americas — the church was the driving force in this process. In Central and South America is seen the evidence of the combination traditions of the settlers and the natives in some of the earliest colonial buildings. Gothic was one of the earliest of the European styles to have a great effect throughout the Americas, chiefly imported by Spanish and Portuguese settlers, from the ornate Mexico City Metropolitan Cathedral (1563) to Sao Francisco at Ouro Preto (1738–1814).

In North America it was slightly different. To begin with, the Catholic Church had less influence; second the notion of local architecture was less obvious as there were fewer permanent structures; finally, the initial ambitions of the first colonizers were limited: they fled persecution in their home countries and came to settle rather than subjugate. In what became the United States, once permanent structures began to be erected, however, it was the classical approach that found favor with the established and prosperous settlers.

Just as in Europe there were key figures in the United States who interpreted the architecture through study and visits to Europe. After serving as ambassador at Versailles, Thomas Jefferson introduced America to Classicism. After creating his own Palladian villa at Monticello, Charlottesville (1770–96), Jefferson, aided by William Thornton and Benjamin Latrobe, went on to plan the University of Virginia (1817–26). Thornton and Latrobe, along with Thomas Ustick Walter, then created one of the iconic buildings of the world — the Capitol in Washington D.C. (1793–1867). The triple-tiara dome by Walter places the building firmly in the 19th century being made of cast iron.

INDUSTRIAL REVOLUTION

A different kind of society began to emerge in the 19th century; the American colonies had won their independence, the French Revolution had been and gone, and more importantly for architecture and building, the Industrial Revolution was underway. Having taken shape in Britain, it spread across Europe, to the Americas and eventually on to the rest of the world. The revolution started with the exploitation of natural resources, especially the power of water and the coal industry. One of its immediate byproducts was massive urbanization as workers flocked to industrial centers; this in turn led to a building boom to house the industries, house the workers and to provide the necessary civic and municipal buildings.

The styles of the day were Classical and Gothic, though there were plenty of other fashions to choose. Influential in this time of change was the writer and critic John Ruskin who wrote *Seven Lamps of Architecture* (1849), a book that would influence the wider appreciation of architecture. In England, the architecture of the Industrial Revolution was Gothic Revival — as is so well exemplified in the Houses of Parliament (1836–51), by Charles Barry and A. W. N. Pugin.

At its completion, the iron frame of the Eiffel Tower was the tallest in the world and still remains today the tallest in Paris.

As the leading authority on Gothic, Pugin designed hundreds of churches, cathedrals and houses as well as being a scholar on the subject. He promoted two principles of architecture: that buildings should have no unnecessary features and that their ornamentation should express the essential structure of the building. St. Giles, Cheadle, shows clearly his intentions for architecture and is the best surviving example of his many churches. Pugin's influence was far reaching, as exemplified by the work of the prolific architect George Gilbert Scott, whose Gothic St. Pancras Station and Hotel is one of London's great pieces of architecture. The rest of the station behind, a soaring vault of cast-iron and glass, was designed by the engineer W. H. Barlow, and contrasted vividly with Scott's Gothic frontage. Here was a new technology in use — a technology not welcomed by Pugin and his followers who strongly opposed it.

Fluid forms of Gaudi's residential work has a sense of growing from the site, his influence can even be seen in the art of H. R. Giger.

The transformation of building technology was the major change brought by the Industrial Revolution, the key areas being new man-made materials, structural techniques, and technical services — particularly in the use of metals (specifically iron). The structural possibilities of iron were first demonstrated at the turn of the 18th century by the great engineers Telford, Stephenson and Brunel, through their railways, bridges, roads, canals, and ships. Iron not only allowed greater flexibility for structures, but also led to new techniques in prefabrication that would alter the craftsmanship of various trades. Another byproduct of this age were the large building contractors who could cope with the new scale of work and who squeezed out the traditional small craft firms.

The Great Exhibition of 1851, housed in Joseph Paxton's Crystal Palace, brought all the new-found techniques together. This building was an indicator of what was achievable and pointed the way to the future in its use of prefabricated materials. Uniquely, it had no real conventional style, did not have restrictions to its size, was light and transparent in a way impossible to produce using brick or stone, and, strikingly when compared with past buildings, the construction took just nine months and could be dismantled and reassembled.

Other major changes of the age were in the way that buildings were planned and in the science of architecture itself. Greater controls were exercised over building work; more architects were trained; the science, being better understood and taught, allowed architectural functions to be clearly delineated and defined. An excellent example of this new age can be found in Paris's Opéra, by Charles Garnier, which showed brilliance of planning, every function thought through and then expressed in sculptural Baroque.

The exploitation of structure epitomized French architecture of the 19th century, Eugène Viollet-le-Duc disclosed in his writings how structural technology could be interpreted and developed in the Gothic style. Henri Labrouste created fine rooms such as the reading rooms of Bibliothèque Nationale (1843–50) through his effective use of iron, but it was the engineer Gustave Eiffel who created the icon of Paris, and the apotheosis of ironwork — the Eiffel Tower. For many years the tallest structure in the world, it was an illustration of elegance and economy, signalling possibilities in both structure and decoration.

BIRTH OF THE SKYSCRAPER

Arguably the most distinctive and enthralling period in architecture — the late 18th and early 20th century — saw new types of building that changed not only the way towns and cities looked but also the very nature of daily lives. In America in the 1880s and 1890s an architectural revolution was under way, led particularly from Chicago, which became the focal point after the devastating fire of 1871. The entire center of this wealthy city was destroyed, providing a design and construction opportunity of unusual and unprecedented size in the modern era. The new buildings set the scene for a modern movement, that would become known as the Chicago School. Its earliest proponent was Henry Hobson who worked for Labrouste in Paris, and developed a style that would act as a model for not only the new generation of architects from Chicago, but eventually all over the world.

It was the skyscraper that defined this era and to this day the taller the building the greater the statement of wealth and power. The first skyscraper was William le Baron Jenney's Home Insurance Building (1883–85). After this, a succession of firms (Burnham and Root, Holabird and Roche, Adler and Sullivan) effectively established the Chicago School world-wide. In Louis Sullivan there emerged a figure who really understood the driving principles of 19th century theorists, that "form follows function," and would display not only an appreciation of logic but, through decorative elements and touches of fantasy, an appreciation of beauty. Not all Sullivan's contemporaries or successors would combine these two essential elements of modern architecture.

Instrumental in the skyscraper's development were key technological developments, such as the invention of the elevator in 1852, made available more widely in 1880, that allowed architects to build up higher while retaining the accessibility of a low rise. More importantly, steel and reinforced concrete — the two building materials essential for the new forms and large spaces of modern architecture — became readily available.

The progression of the work of the Chicago School was realized by Auguste Perret, whose apartments at 25bis rue Franklin, Paris (1903), showed that concrete frames made unnecessary the use of load-bearing walls. It was Perret that gave the new material respectability. Also influential was Anatole de Bardot's church of St.-Jean-de-Montmartre in Paris (1897–1904), which eliminated anything deemed unnecessary to the structure, but with a touch of fantasy in the decorative detailings.

The spiral ramp of the Guggenheim is not conducive to displaying art at its best. But it is this form that gives it its magnificence and has made Frank lloyd Wright's building an icon.

The decorative style that evolved in Paris was Art Nouveau, the leading exponent of which was Hector Guimard who designed the entrances for the Paris Metro in 1900. In the same way that the Victorians used Gothic Revival as personal expression, so too did the followers of Art Nouveau, exploring decorative themes in abstracted biological and botanical motifs. The initiator of the style was Victor Horta, who set about creating interiors with a stylistic unity of flowing curves and decorative wrought iron. The use of a variety of materials both externally and internally suggested an organic nature, but this rarely translated well into anything other than a decorative style for specific buildings. An exception to this came in the work of the Catalonian architect Antoni Gaudi, whose originality in Modernismo (Art Nouveau in Spain) still fascinates today. The forms of Gaudi, as seen in the unfinished cathedral Sagrada Familia, Barcelona and other projects, can all be traced back to nature; the paraboloid, the hyperboloid and the helicoid. Gaudi took great care with forms, ensuring they were both structurally sound and geometrically precise.

Introduced to Britain via the illustrations of Aubrey Beardsley, Art Nouveau had been influenced by the functional approach of the Arts and Craft Movement. William Morris had taken the principles of Pugin and Ruskin and added the belief that architecture was the expression of society. Through Morris and the likes of Philip Webb, who designed Morris's own home Red House, London (1859–60), a direction was established pointing to the virtues of using materials truthfully. The Arts and Craft Movement enjoyed the traditional forms of native architecture and of craftwork made from natural materials; prominent advocates of these ideals were architects such as Charles Annesley Voysey and Richard Norman Shaw, but it was Edwin Lutyens who became the most successful, with more than a hundred houses and several large projects such as the Viceroy's House in New Delhi. The evolutions in town planning in the 19th century would become a preoccupation of Lutyens.

Le Corbusieris elegant white box raised on pilotis has recently undergone a much-needed refurbishment; the lower form was derived from the turning circle of a car.

In Scotland Charles Rennie Mackintosh promoted a Scottish style of Art Nouveau that demonstrated his overall mastery of materials. His major work was the Glasgow School of Art where he did all the details, the light fittings, the door furniture, the windows and the periodical tables, and his work spawned a host of imitators. An attaché to the German embassy in London, Herman Methesius's book *Das englische Haus* (1904–05), described the leading figures in the English Arts and Crafts Movement. This influence can be seen in Joseph Maria Olbrich's exhibition hall at Darmstadt (1907) and, more expressively, in Otto Wagner's Post Office Savings Bank (1904–06). At the extreme end of this functionalism was Adolf Loos who wrote in 1908 an article on Ornament and Crime insisting on the complete elimination of ornamentation from useful objects.

This expressive period produced one definitive genius, whom many regard (as he did himself) as the greatest architect of the 20th century: Frank Lloyd Wright. A protege of Louis Sullivan, he not only outlived the Chicago School but would play an influential part in several major styles which followed; his influence can still be felt today. His great array of work spanned 70 years and is a remarkable study of the use of a variety of materials — especially steel, local stone, concrete and wood. His early houses were domestic undertakings, many around his own home and studio — an excellent showcase of his work — in Oak Park, Chicago. The form of these results from the crossing of axes, the flow of internal spaces, and change of levels defining spaces without the use of doors or walls. His later Prairie Houses created the "open plan" building, his most memorable and best known being the Robie House (1908–09). Wright illustrates composition rather the use of technology, and the plan and the flow of the spaces changed forever the concept of the house. Wright also excelled in man-made forms complementing nature, as can be seen in the iconic Fallingwater at Bear Run, Pennsylvania (1935–37) and Taliesin West at Phoenix, Arizona (1938), both of which show succinctly his concepts of organic architecture.

The 20 years either side of the turn of the century produced an architecture that had an international conception but allowed great local diversity in interpretation. World War 1 changed attitudes and this had a reflection in architecture's new phase of uniformity, best represented by the International Style.

THE INTERNATIONAL STYLE

A term coined in 1932 by Philip Johnson and Henry Russell Hitchcock, the organizers of the First International Exhibition of Modern Architecture in New York, the subsequent book stated:

> *"There is, first, a new conception of architecture as volume rather than mass. Secondly, regularity rather than axial symmetry serves as the chief means of ordering design."*

It was order that the designers and planners required in the turmoil of the early 20th century. Architecture was seen as a catalyst to social change, and for the first time the welfare of society became an instrument for great architecture. The figure that stood out in this new movement was a founding member of an influential group, the Congrès Internationaux d'Architecture Moderne (CIAM). He was Charles Edouard Jeanneret, better known as "Le Corbusier." His first book, *Vers une architecture* (1927), highlights his anxiousness to create the idyllic society and announcing the five points of a new architecture: free standing supports (*pilotis*), the roof garden, the open plan, the ribbon window and the freely composed façade. His interpretation of objects was akin to the Cubist painters, with Domino House, a simple diagram expressing the freedom of plan and façade.

A magnificent and iconistic structure of New York City, the Chrysler Building remains one of the finest — if not the finest — example of the Art Deco style.

Le Corbusier's "Modular Man," a precise formula for satisfactory proportions, became the basis of the scale he applied to the construction of any building. Based on the human body and the golden section (very reminiscent of the system employed by Renaissance architects such as Alberti), Modular could be used on any scale as shown in Villa Savoye (1928–31) and the huge mass housing project, Unité d'Habitation, Marseilles. Even when producing the seemingly irregular Nôtre-Dame-du-Haut, Ronchamp (1950–54), all the dimensions were controlled by Modular and the planning based on a series of right angles. Another preoccupation was the manipulation of space with light: "architecture is the masterly, correct and magnificent play of volumes brought together in light."

In Germany the movement had defined divisions, expressive and sculptural as seen in Erich Mendelsohn's Einstein Tower, Potsdam (1919–21) and the more formal style of Walter Gropius and Adolf Meyer's Fagus Factory at Alfeld-an-der-Leine (1911). It was Gropius who established the Bauhaus School of Design in 1919; it taught design, building and craftsmanship with the likes of Klee, Wassily and Kandinsky on the staff. Their principles are clear to see in the Bauhaus's own buildings in Dessau, Germany (1925–26), which present a changing sequence of solid and transparent spaces articulating specific functions. His teaching had an influential effect worldwide, especially through Ludwig Mies van der Rohe, (his successor as the head of the Bauhaus) who took his teachings on to America.

In 1917 a similar group emerged in Leiden, the Netherlands, called *De Stijl* (The Style); their architecture consisted of interlocking geometric forms and primary colors, and they drew their inspiration from the work of the artist Piet Mondrian. The Schroder House, Utrecht (1923–04) by Gerrit Rietveld is the outstanding example of the De Stijl aesthetics.

Succeeding on a troubled site in terms of location, the Royal Festival Hall works, thanks to a creative solution in isolating the auditorium from the external noise and vibrations of the nearby railway lines going into Waterloo Station.

A number of refugees from the Continent showed examples of the International Style in Britain, the house High and Over at Amersham (1929–30) by Amyas Connell being the first. Gropius, before going to America, spent time in Britain where he worked with the young Maxwell Fry on the Sunhouse in Hampshire (1936), but the greatest impact in British International Style was by the Russian émigré, Bernard Lubetkin in projects like the Penguin Pool at London Zoo (1934), Highpoint I and II at Highgate London (1933–38). It wasn't until after World War 2, however, that the International Style in Britain began to flourish. London County Council's architects' office led the way creating public buildings to this style — the centerpiece for the Festival of Britain in 1951, the Royal Festival Hall, and public housing such as the Council Housing blocks at Roehampton, Surrey. Before the war Scandinavia too, had readily accepted the International Style in all forms of buildings; here the work of Alvar Aalto stood out, inspired by the landscape he managed to make his architecture humane, expressive and romantic, while still retaining local vernacular qualities.

As in Britain, the United States's first buildings in the style, such as Rudolf Schindler's Lovell Beach House at Newport Beach (1925–26), were designed by Europeans. It would be after the Wall Street crash of 1929 — but more particularly after World War 2 — that the style took shape through commercial buildings. During the 1930s, some remarkable buildings were constructed in New York, the Art Deco Chrysler Building (1928–30), the Empire State Building (1930–32) and the Rockefeller Center (1930-40) to name but three.

Mies van der Rohe was a supreme influence not only through his own buildings but also through his American students. Philip Johnson showed he had understood and learnt from the teachings of Mies when he created his own home in New Canaan (1949). The first architectural realization of Mies's early vision of glass skyscrapers came through the seminal office building, Lever House (1951–52) by Skidmore, Owings and Merrill. The last major work of the style came from the partnership of Mies and Johnson in the form of the Seagram Building in New York.

As a consultant on the design of the new Ministry of Education building in Rio de Janeiro (1936), Le Corbusier was again able to spread his influence. Brazil after World War 2 saw an architectural explosion, the newly planned capital Brasilia displaying a purity of geometry on a scale not witnessed before and bringing the work of Oscar Niemeyer to prominence. Thought to be a total architecture, International Modern rejected everything that had gone before but turned out, eventually, to be just a style like the preceding styles.

LATE TWENTIETH CENTURY

The arrogance of the founders of the International Style in their belief that, after thousands of years, they had devised the definitive style of architecture was the underlying cause for the style's demise. Highlighted by the demolition of Pruitt Igoe flats in St. Louis, designed by Minoru Yamasaki in 1955 and previously decorated by the American Institute of Architects, the failure of the social housing projects marked how much times had changed. Mass housing and office development, which made up the majority of the International Style buildings, were criticised by the people who used them.

Architecture went in many directions, with no single style dominant: whether this is for better or worse only time will tell. Certainly it has led to uncomplementary buildings being placed next to each other, a plethora of revival styles and anything with an "-ism" —Traditionalism, Brutalism, Constructivism, Expressionism, Futurism, Historicism, Metabolism, Neo-Metabolism, the New Empiricism, Organicism, Post-modernism and Utilitarian Functualism. Today's architecture can be described best as Pluralism and on the evidence of the last 30 years it looks set to stay. When all is said and done, however, this state of flux has produced some of the most remarkable architecture ever.

Possibly the most important building of the late 20th century, Frank Gehry's Guggenheim is an exciting harbinger of the architecture of the 21st century.

Developments in technology and, most significantly, materials used in structural design have advanced dramatically. External forces and their consequential knock-on effects have altered the shape of buildings. The prefabrication of materials and whole sections of a building have changed architects' methodology. Technical services have also improved, as have the demands by the users who now want far higher levels of comfort.

When despondent architects started to realize that the views of the pioneers of the International Style were not reflected in the users of their buildings, many deliberately went against the grain. The bird-like TWA Terminal at JFK International Airport (1956–62) by Eero Saarinen, constructed in reinforced concrete, altered people's perception of what could be achieved. Designers started composing dramatic buildings but with more thought about the functions of the building and its users. Progression came in Robert Venturi's book *Complexity and Contradiction in Architecture* (1966), seeking architecture of meaning. A clear example of the complex, unexpected and metaphorical language of his school is communicated in his mother's house at Chestnut Hill, Philadelphia (1962–64).

Adventure was the order of the day; fun and complexity quickly replaced the simplicity of the International Style. Architects still called on the past, but often almost as sound bites of the past, in-jokes between architects. Architecture became disposable and plastic, a reflection of the society of consumerism. Nobody represents this style better than Charles Moore whose Piazza d'Italia, New Orleans (1975–78) was a grand polychromatic building that unashamedly exhibited kitsch. New small projects in Los Angeles also showed this flamboyancy, but unlike the Post-modern Classicism of Moore and Michael Graves, the young architects in L.A. worked in a very insular area where their particular brand of architecture only gradually revealed itself as one of the most provocative to emerge. Some of the most extraordinary examples of the architectural free-for-all now being experienced were clearly visible in the World Exposition of 1967 in Montreal; it was here that Buckminster Fuller displayed a geodesic dome and Moshe Safdie created the Habitat Housing.

Petronas Towers. At the end of the 20th century the twin towers hold the much coveted title of being the world's tallest building. Luckily it was finished before the great Far Eastern financial crash, when seemingly the power of money could achieve anything.

Europe, too, joined in producing buildings that still remain fascinating today, the likes of Hans Scharoun's Philharmonic Concert Hall, Berlin (1956–63), a solution to acoustical problems, expressing a rational but irregular form. Innovations in new materials allowed the forms that were previously not possible: Frei Otto in partnership with Günter Behnisch presented the world with a spectacular tented roof for the Munich Games of 1972.

Britain showed a great deal of reluctance to journey down this path; Peter and Alison Smithson, like many, stuck firmly to the beliefs in Le Corbusier's way of thinking in the Economist (1962–64) Building; James Stirling and James Gowan's Engineering Building, Leicester owed more to the past than the current climate abroad. All this would soon change as a handful of pioneers celebrated the technology available: leaders of this High-Tech movement were Norman Foster and Richard Rogers, who started out together and followed similar paths. The buildings they created for large commercial companies showed great faith in new technology and became instant icons — Willis Faber and Dumas, Ipswich (1974), Hong Kong and Shanghai Bank, Hong Kong (1979–86), Lloyds of London (1978–86) and Centre Pompidou (1971–77).

The rise in economic power of the Far East, especially Japan, was mirrored in experimentation in architecture. The breadth of their imagination seemed boundless and, indeed, contemporary architecture of the region would, in its turn, influence the West.

One of today's styles, however, certainly does confound the observer and challenge conventions on how spaces should be arranged — Deconstructivism, grounded in the chaos of of Los Angeles. Initially restricted to southern California, many of its proponents have grown in reputation, although few as much as the "Godfather" of the style, Frank O. Gehry. With huge commissions from multi-national companies, Gehry has created incredible structures such as the Guggenheim Museum, Bilbao (1997).

Today there is still no definitive architectural style, perhaps there need not be a controlling style, we need to learn that certain typologies require different treatments, and in this age we may just be able to live in an era undefined by any particular style.

THE DIGITAL MILLENNIUM

Throughout history architects have drawn their inspiration from the work and theories of the past; the lessons learnt from bad as well as good architecture reinforce subsequent progression. Since the establishment of basic construction techniques, very little has changed in the fundamental principles. What the observer sees and ultimately passes judgement on is the decoration a particular style projects. Architecture does not exist in a vacuum; styles do not evolve solely from one to the next. As in any creative field the creator uses the experiences of the changing world alongside the study of past architecture. What is clearly evident is that, as construction techniques improve, styles become more complex and dynamic.

Styles of the past always had long periods of development — the Egyptians kept their distinct style for thousands of years with very little change. But the pace of technology and communications in the modern world has had the effect of reducing the length of a style's period and, ultimately, ensuring style diversity. Greater documentation of the past has lead to the reinterpretation of what we previously assumed to be true; for example, few realized that the Greeks and Egyptians used garish colors on and in their buildings.

It is impossible to know what the future holds, but there are always telltale signs to what the future could hold. Architecture needs to realize where it wants to be by the end of the next century and make positive steps to succeed. This means that certain old traits and habitats will inevitably have to be discarded to make way for growth. Some forward-thinking architects believe that radical changes are called for now, and the sooner the better. These changes would not be merely superficial but alter the fundamentals of architecture. One such architect is Neil Spiller, diploma tutor at the Bartlett (UCL), whose book *Digital Dreams: Architecture and the New Alchemic Technologies* explores new possibilities in architecture and the failures of the current situation.

Technologies that can radically reprogram plant and animal cells can be used to create numerous proteins that have potential as building materials. Recent successes in tissue engineering with growing bone cultures suggest the potential of bone as a new structural material. Indeed, we have already reached the stage where we can postulate the ultimate technology: nanotechnology. Nanotechnology is truly alchemic engineering and magical in its potential. It could give humanity the power to manipulate matter atom by atom, thereby changing one material into another. The architectural future is more exciting than ever . . .

The largest dome in the world. Political problems aside, the architecture of the dome is a pure high-tech solution of simplicity and drama.

THE BUILDINGS

Sagrada Familia, Barcelona, Spain (started 1884)

Gaudi lived for the last part of his life in the crypt of his unfinished masterpiece.
Photographer: John Edward Linden/1206:790

CAVE DWELLINGS, GOREME, TURKEY (PREHISTORIC)

Original settlements for the indigenous Europeans, before wood techniques were developed.

Photographer: Nick Meers/5161:20

CAVE DWELLINGS, GOREME, TURKEY (PREHISTORIC)

The harsh environment of this region led to entire villages being carved out of the surrounding hills.
Photographer: Nick Meers/5161:10

Stepped Pyramid of King Zoser, Sakkara, Egypt (c. 2630–2610 BC)

Imhotep

The six-stepped pyramid, 200 feet high, was the last stage before the geometrically true pyramid.

Photographer: Peter Brown/1770:10

Pyramids of Giza, Egypt (c. 2550–2470 BC)

The best known of the pyramids is that of the pharaoh Khufu. It is orientated precisely to the four points of the compass with sides of near exact equilateral triangles set at an angle of 51–52 degrees.

Photographer: Farrel Grehan/4700:80

THE SPHYNX, GIZA, EGYPT (BEFORE 3700 BC)

Shrouded in mystery for years, the Sphinx was eventually unearthed in 1816 AD by Caviglia. In the form of a semi-recumbent lion, it is 65 feet high and 150 feet long; between its paws lies a sacrificial altar.

Photographer: Farrel Grehan/4701:30

PYRAMIDS OF GIZA, EGYPT, AT SUNSET (C. 2550–2470 BC)

The triad of great pyramids at Giza are the monuments to the pharaohs of the Fourth Dynasty (2613–2498BC), Khufu, Kephren and Menkaure. That of Menkaure has three smaller pyramids of his queens at its feet

Photographer: Farrel Grehan/4700:90

Temple of Amun-Ra, Luxor, Thebes, Egypt (c.1460–c. 320 BC)

Typical monumental massing of an Egyptian temple; the great open outer court contrasts with the covered hypostyle hall with its 134 papyrus-bud columns.

Photographer: Peter Brown/1774:30

OSIRIS PILLARS, THE RAMESSEUM AT THE TEMPLE OF AMUN-RA, LUXOR, THEBES, EGYPT (C. 1460–C. 320 BC)

Commenced by Amenophis III and dedicated to the Theban triad Amun, Mut and Khons, Ramesses II was responsible for many additions to the temple.

Photographer: Peter Brown/1774:30

TEMPLE OF HORUS, EDFU, EGYPT (237 BC)

Detail of a composite capital, formed of rings of lotus flowers and volutes, from the colonnade that sits behind the massive pylon.
Photographer: Peter Brown/1775:20

THE HERAION, OLYMPIA, GREECE (C. 640 BC)

Believed to be the most ancient of all the Greek temples discovered, the Heraion stands on a stylobate of two steps, measuring 168 feet by 641/2 feet. The original oak columns decayed and were replaced by either stone monoliths or built-up stone drums.

Photographer: Farrel Grehan/4761:40

TEMPLE OF POSEIDON, PAESTUM, ITALY (C. 450 BC)

Built of coarse travertine stone, in which are fossil plants and aqueous weeds, the stone was originally covered in fine stucco. This is the only existing temple with an internal colonnade of Doric columns.

Photographer: Farrel Grehan/4762:20

THE ERECHTHEION, ATHENS, GREECE (C. 420–393 BC)

Mnesicle

Detail of the Ionic order of The Erechtheion, which was regarded with veneration as it contained memorials connected with the religion of the state.

Photographer: Colin Dixon/4817:20

Temple of Tholos, Delphi, Greece (c. 510 BC)

A dramatic unity of nature and gods, the circular temple of this sacred site guides the traveller towards the slopes of Parnassus, where the shrine of Apollo sits.

Photographer: Natalie Tepper/4748.10

PARTHENON ACROPOLIS, ATHENS, GREECE (447–432 BC)

Ictinus and Callicartes

Best known of the Greek buildings, a study in perfection of form and proportion. The Parthenon's optical illusions are not limited to the columns; all the horizontals have been corrected to avoid the appearance of sagging.

Photographer: Peter Brown/1765:10

Temple of Apollo, Didymeus (near Miletus), Turkey (c. 450 BC)

This hypethral temple is a dipteral decastyle: architectural terminology for a temple that is open to the sky and surrounded by double rows of columns and with two ranges of ten at either end.

Photographer: Natalie Tepper/4936:10

CARYATID PORCH, ERECHTHEUM, ACROPOLIS, ATHENS, GREECE (C. 421–406 BC)

Powerfully built maidens, known as Caryatids, replace traditional columns in the porch of the Erechtheum. Controversially they,too, have been replaced — by fibre-glass casts due to pollution erosion.

Photographer: Colin Dixon/4817:10

CARYATID PORCH, ERECHTHEUM, ACROPOLIS, ATHENS, GREECE (C. 421–406 BC)

Detail of the Caryatid columns of the porch.
Photographer: Robert O'Dea/1765:40

MAISON CARRÉE, NÎMES, FRANCE (C. 16 BC)

The best-preserved Roman temple to be found, this view shows four of the six Corinthian columns at the front supporting a rich entablature. Behind can be seen the portico

Photographer: John Edward Linden/5300:10

Roman Baths, Avon, England (c. 1 AD)

Naturally hot spring water still gushes up and flows through the massive leaden conduit into the great swimming bath.
Photographer: John Edward Linden/1540:20

THE LIBRARY OF THE ANCIENT RUINS, EPHESUS, TURKEY (C. 356 BC)

A major centre of the Greek and Roman Asiatic colonies, Ephesus once had a population of 300,000.
Photographer: Nick Meers/830:120

THE COLOSSEUM, ROME, ITALY (82 AD)

Vespasian

Built to a vast elliptical plan, 620 feet by 513 feet, with 80 external arcaded openings on each storey, the Flavian Amphitheatre was started by the Emperor Vespasian and completed by Domitian.

Photographer: Richard Glover/4011:90

THE COLOSSEUM, ROME, ITALY (82 AD)

Vespasian

The arena is an oval, 287 feet by 180 feet, with room for some 50,000 spectators. Beneath there are corridors and stairs, while under the lowest tier, on a level with the arena floor, are dens for the wild animals.

Photographer: Richard Glover/4011:80

PUENTE ROMANA (ROMAN BRIDGE), CORDOBA, SPAIN (C. 100 AD)

Typical of many Roman Bridges, the simple, solid and practical construction was designed to offer well-calculated resistance to the rush of water. Found throughout the Roman Empire, bridges were key to the spread of civilisation.

Photographer: Colin Dixon/4336:30

Roman Theatre, Aspendos, Turkey (c.100 AD)

Theatres are characteristically Roman buildings, found in every major important settlement.
Photographer: Natalie Tepper/4935:10

The Theatre, Orange, France (c. 50 AD)

Partly constructed and partly hollowed out of the hillside, this theatre holds 7,000 spectators. The wall of the outer façade is ornamented with wall arcading.

Photographer: Mark Fiennes/7232:10

PANTHEON, ROME, ITALY (C. 120–124 AD)

The Pantheon, the temple of the gods, built by the Emperor Hadrian, has a dome diameter of 143 feet, which remained the widest dome in the world until the 19th century. The dome is perfectly formed, a hemisphere whose radius is equal to its height.

Photographers: Peter Brown/1771:10

Pantheon, Rome, Italy (c. 120–124 AD)

Rear view of the Pantheon giving a better idea of the diameter of the dome.
Photographers: Richard Glover/1771:100

Arch of Septimus Severus, Rome, Italy (c. 204 AD)

Celebrating the Parthian victories of the emperor and his two sons, the white marble triumphal arch has the typical adornment of statuary and bas-reliefs of the victorious campaign.

Photographer: Richard Glover/5124:10

The Basilica of Constantine, Rome, Italy (c. 310–313 AD)

Also known as the Basilica of Maxentius or the Temple of Peace, the Basilica of Constantine consists of a central nave, 265 feet long by 83 feet wide, and was crowned with a 120-foot groined vault in three compartments.

Photographer: Richard Glover/5122:10

Novodevichi Convent, Moscow, Russia (c. 1500)

Included out of chronological sequence, this Moscow convent exemplifies Byzantine architecture that proliferated in Russia as a result of the strong trade links established between the Byzantines and Kievan Russia. The Russians added to the style the onion dome that swells outwards before curving inwards to a point.

Photographer: Alan Williams/2189:20

ST BASIL'S CATHEDRAL, RED SQUARE MOSCOW, RUSSIA (C. 1550-60)

Built by Ivan the Terrible in celebration of his victories, the cathedral has since been decorated with coloured tiles that give an oriental appearance.

Photographer: Alex Bartel/2962:30

San Miniato al Monte, Florence, Italy (c. 1018–62)

A departure from the typical basilican architecture of the classical period — characterised by long unbroken ranges of columns and arches, this Romanesque church is divided by piers into three main compartments.
Photographer: Richard Bryant/2226:20

San Miniato al Monte, Florence, Italy (c. 1018–62)

Translucent marble of the sanctuary is used in place of glass in the window openings. The open timber roof, with its bright colour decoration, displays the simple basilican style of roof.

Photographer: Richard Bryant/2226:60

San Miniato al Monte, Florence, Italy (c. 1018-62)

Detail of the exterior decoration, showing the local custom of skilled use of brick with marble facings.
Photographer: Richard Bryant/2226:40

THE CATHEDRAL AND BAPTISTERY, PISA, ITALY (C. 1063–1272)

One of the finest Romanesque buildings, the cathedral has strong individuality althoughits plan has many of the traits of earlier basilican churches. Rising one above another, the open arches of the entrance façade have a delicate ornamentation and beauty.

Photographer: Robert O'Dea/8087:30

THE CAMPANILE, PISA, ITALY (C. 1174)

The world-famous leaning tower rises in eight storeys of encircling arcades, with its upper part overhanging its base by as much as 14 feet, thus giving it an unstable appearance, something emphasised by this photographic angle..

Photographer: Robert O'Dea/8088:10

The Baptistery, Pisa, Italy (c. 1153–1272)

Dioti Salvi

The exterior articulated by engaged columns on the ground storey — which includes four portals — Salvi's Baptistery has a vaulted interior. The arcade is surmounted by 14th century Gothic additions which disguises the original design

Photographer: Robert O'Dea/8089:30:1

SANTA MARIA DELLA ASSUNTA, TORCELLO, VENICE, ITALY (C.1350)

The characteristic campanile of this late Romanesque church, typical of many in Northern Italy, stood as more of a civic monument than integral part of the church.

Photographer: Ian Lambot/410:20

CA'D'ORO, PALAZZO, GRAND CANAL, VENICE, ITALY (C. 1422–40)

A palatial home of a merchant prince, the Venetian mannered grouping of windows form the centre of the façade. An arcaded entrance lights the deep central hall.

Photographer: Alex Bartel/5143:10

Sienna Cathedral, Santa Maria Della Assunta, Sienna, Italy (c. 1245–1380)

Largely the outcome of civic pride, Sienna cathedral was a stupendous undertaking involving all the artists of the region contributing to the building and its adornment.

Photographer: David Fowler/2340:140

THE DUOMO, FLORENCE, ITALY (C. 1396–1462)

Arnolfo di Cambio, Brunelleschi and others

Essentially Italian in character and lacking the vertical features of north Italy, the Duomo was built around the old church of Santa Reparata. The famous dome was the design of Brunelleschi and took over 16 years to construct. The lantern was added after Brunelleschi's death.

Photographer: Robert O'Dea/2222:170

The Duomo, Florence, Italy (c. 1396–1462)

Arnolfo di Cambio, Brunelleschi and others

The marble facing of the west façade was not entirely completed until 1887.

Photographer: Robert O'Dea/2222:190

GRAND CANAL, VENICE, ITALY

A typical view of Venice, unchanged for centuries, with a mixture of the Romanesque, the Gothic and the Renaissance.

Photographer: Ian Lambot/1112:10

HOTEL DANIELI, VENICE, ITALY (15TH CENTURY)

The Hotel Danieli demonstrates the typical attributes of Venetian Gothic — arched windows on each storey central to the façade, with several arched openings and protruding balconies on either side.

Photographer: Ian Lambot/1110:10

DANIELI

MILAN CATHEDRAL, MILAN, ITALY (C. 1385–1485)

Milan cathedral, with its distinctive flèche (wooden spire), was erected by the first Duke of Milan. A gleaming mass of white marble with traceried windows, panelled buttresses, flying buttresses and pinnacles topped with statutes, it is the only true example of the Gothic in Italy.

Photographer: John Croce/2232:10

SANTA MARIA NOVELLA, FLORENCE, ITALY (C. 1278–1350; FAÇADE 1456–70)

The original design of the exterior can be seen in the blind arcading on the entrance façade, — completed later by Alberti during the Renaissance.

Photographer: Richard Bryant/2225:20

Bourges Cathedral, France (c. 1190–1275)

Resembling the plan of Nôtre Dame in Paris, Bourges cathedral lacks transepts, the nave has triforium, a clear-storey and a sexpartie vault 125 feet high. Innumerable double flying buttresses over the aisles of the east end allow the near full glazing of the walls revealing some of the best stained glass in France.

Photographer: Mark Fiennes/900:20

VOTIV CHURCH (VOTIVKIRCHE), VIENNA, AUSTRIA (C. 1856–1879)

A marvelous example of Gothic architecture inspired by the cathedral of Cologne, Votiv Church is noted for its distinctive double spires with their intricate design. The church was commissioned by Maximilian, the Emperor of Mexico, from the architect Heinrich Freiherr von Ferstel.

Photographer: Gisela Erlacher/4042:80

Antwerp Cathedral, Belgium (c. 1352–1411)

The largest church in Belgium, the single monumental tower on the west front (403½ feet) has a companion tower terminated at a lower level. The unusual bulbous turret over the crossing is a remnant of the Spanish occupation.

Photographer: Mark Fiennes/4033:10

BARCELONA CATHEDRAL, BARCELONA, SPAIN (1298–1448)

Designed in the Italian method, the cathedral is vaulted in square in the nave, the aisles in oblong bays. The deep internal buttress counteracts the thrust of the vault, which enclose side chapels along the aisles.

Photographer: Kurwenal/Prisma/4326:10

Mont St. Michel, Normandy, France (c. 1022–1135, rebuilt choir 1456–1521)

Built on a large rock in the bay between Avranches and St-Malo, Mont St. Michel is a fortified monastery with secular as well as monastic buildings. Its walls are all dominated by the "Merveille" and the "Salle de Chevaliers".

Photographer: Alex Bartel/3097:40

NÔTRE DAME CATHEDRAL, PARIS, FRANCE (C. 1163–1235)

One of the oldest of the French Gothic cathedrals, its wide spread western façade has served as a model for many later churches. The three recessed portals are surmounted by a row of statues depicting the kings of France, above which sits the famous wheel window (42 feet diameter).

Photographer: Alex Bartel/2334:90

Nôtre Dame Cathedral, Paris, France (c. 1163–1235)

The east end of Nôtre Dame has some of the best examples of flying buttresses anywhere, giving an ethereal appearance — all finished by a 300-foot flèche.

Photographer: Alex Bartel/2334:40

NÔTRE DAME CATHEDRAL, PARIS, FRANCE (C. 1163–1235)

The cathedral is adorned around the upper part of the western towers with sculptures of animals similar to the gargoyles on other parts.

Photographer: David Churchill/2334:10

SAINTE CHAPELLE, ILE DE LA CÎTÉ, PARIS, FRANCE (C. 1244–47)

This is very small chapel with a delicate flèche and characteristic French features such as the apsidal termination and the high stone-vaulted roof. Windows occupy the spaces between the buttresses, 15 feet by 50 feet, giving a lantern-like quality to the interior.

Photographer: Richard Glover/7113:20

Chartes Cathedral, France (c. 1194–1260)

Still used for pilgrimages to the shrine of the Vierge Noire, Chartres is an unusual French cathedral for the extensive stained glass of its 130 windows and the abundance of sculptured figures in the doorway of the western façade.

Photographer: John Stuart Miller/3875:20

CHATEAU DE BLOIS, LOIRE, FRANCE (C. 1498–1515)

This chateau was built in various styles over some years. The principal feature is an irregular quadrangle with a central entrance built for Louis XII, which is enriched with statues.

Photographer: Colin Dixon/5062:20

Entree

THE WHITE TOWER, TOWER OF LONDON, LONDON, ENGLAND (C. 1078–97)

The White Tower — so named because at one time it was whitewashed — is the central keep, built by William I and William II. Initially used as a fortress to subjugate London, it has since been used as a palace and, more infamously, as a prison.

Photographer: Lark Gilmer/1003:130

Tower of London, London, England (c. 1078–97)

The completed concentric form was only finished after several successive reigns. A wall with 13 towers, that in turn has its own bailey, surrounds the inner bailey, with the whole encircled by a moat.

Photographer: Lark Gilmer/1003:210

WINDSOR CASTLE, BERKSHIRE, ENGLAND (12TH CENTURY)

Still used as a residence by the monarchy, Windsor is typical of the "Shell" keep, erected on existing earthworks, its masonry walls circling the mound on which it was built.

Photographer: Martin Jones/3365:50

GALILEE CHAPEL, TOMB OF THE VENERABLE BEDE, DURHAM CATHEDRAL, COUNTY DURHAM, ENGLAND (C.1093–15)

Historically the most important building of the Anglo-Norman style, Durham is the earliest example of a church constructed throughout with ribbed vaults.

Photographer: Colin Dixon/1253:80

DURHAM CATHEDRAL, COUNTY DURHAM, ENGLAND (C. 1093–15)

Sited on cliffs above the River Wear, Durham cathedral is as spectacular and impressive externally as it is internally.

Photographer: Jeremy Cockayne/1253:30

Canterbury Cathedral, Kent, England (c. 1174–78)

William of Sens, William the Englishman

Adapting the French model, William of Sens erected the choir, which was continued by William the Englishman. A central tower in the Perpendicular style was added later (1490–1530).

Photographer: Martin Jones/2137:60

PETERBOROUGH CATHEDRAL, LINCOLNSHIRE, ENGLAND (C. 1117–90)

The 164-feet wide western façade of Peterborough has three huge arches standing proud of the aisles and nave. The form dominates the architecture, making the decorations secondary; ribbed vaulting is particularly beautifully expressed in the eastern tower.

Photographer: Martine Hamilton Knight/1966

SALISBURY CATHEDRAL, WILTSHIRE, ENGLAND (C. 1220–60)

Boasting the loftiest spire in England at 403½ feet high, Salisbury is unique in being the only English cathedral to be built without interruption in the Middle Ages.

Photographer: Richard Bryant/428:10

WESTMINSTER ABBEY, LONDON, ENGLAND (C. 1245–69)

Built originally in the Norman style, the Abbey saw regular rebuilding, additions and repairs until the end result became Gothic. The two western towers were added even later (c. 1735–40) by John James or Nicholas Hawksmoor.

Photographer: Mark Fdiennes/930:1

Henry VII Chapel (Interior), Westminster Abbey, London, England (c. 1503–19)

Keeping in the Gothic, the Henry VII Chapel has detailed fan-tracery and is one of the finest pendant vaults of the period.
Photographer: Mark Fdiennes/930:50

Wells Cathedral, Somerset, England (c. 1180–1425)

Columns supported by inverted arches take the massive weight of the interior.
Photographer: Martin Jones/1545:40

St. George's Chapel, Windsor Castle, Berkshire, England (c. 1473–1516)

A specially designed Royal mortuary chapel, St. George's Chapel is fan-vaulted, a style confined to England.
Photographer: John Edward Linden/5216:30

KINGS COLLEGE CHAPEL, CAMBRIDGE UNIVERSITY, CAMBRIDGESHIRE, ENGLAND (C. 1446–1515)

In common with many other colleges, Kings College Chapel has heraldic shields with armorial bearings and scroll inscriptions.

Photographer: Martin Jones/2041:70

HAMPTON COURT PALACE, SURREY, ENGLAND (C, 1515–30)

Built by Cardinal Wolsey, the Tudor palace is famed for provoking the envy of Henry VIII — until the cardinal had no option but to hand it over to him. The diaper-pattern red-brick façade has battlement parapets which are strewn with Tudor chimneys — all magnificent examples of the brick architecture of the time.

Photographer: David Churchill/1005

LITTLE MORETON HALL, CHESHIRE, ENGLAND (C. 1550-59)

Erected by newly wealthy trading families, the manor house of the early sixteenth century is primarily Tudor. However, with its long gallery (75 feet by 12½ feet) Little Morton Hall is often regarded as an early Renaissance building.

Photographer: Clay Perry/1508:10

Santa Maria De Donato, Murano, Venice, Italy
(15th century)

The Renaissance architecture of Venice merged with the existing Gothic to produce a distinct character, and the transition between the two styles produced a culmination of both not surpassed anywhere else.

Photographer: Ian Lambot/408:10

La Rotunda — Villa Capra, Vicenza, Italy (c. 1565–69)

Andrea Palladio

A precise and exact classical example, Villa Capra (Rotunda) displays both controlled classical rules and Albert's Rules and spirit. The villa has been the model for many that followed and still stands as a benchmark.

Photographer: Richard Bryant/2024:20

La Rotunda — Villa Capra, Vicenza, Italy (c. 1565–69)

Andrea Palladio

Almost perfectly symmetrical in plan, the Rotunda is based around a circular room covered by a dome. Pillared porticoes on each side are approached by even flights of stairs, giving a similar appearance from any direction.

Photographer: Richard Bryant/2024:80

San Giorgio Maggiore, Venice, Italy (c. 1566–1610)

Andrea Palladio

On an island in the lagoon, San Giorgio Maggiore presents a magnificent silhouette of dome, turrets and a very tall campanile.

Photographer: Ian Lambot/406:30

San Giorgio Maggiore, Venice, Italy (c. 1566–1610)

Andrea Palladio

The façade, completed by Scamozzi (1575), displays the adaptation of Classics Orders to the basic church.

Photographer: Ian Lambot/406:20

San Giorgio Maggiore, Venice, Italy (c. 1566–1610)

Andrea Palladio

An internal courtyard surrounded by a classical arcade backs onto San Giorgio Maggiore.

Photographer: Ian Lambot/406:60

ST. PETER'S SQUARE, THE VATICAN, ROME, ITALY (1506–1626)

Bramante, Raphael, Peruzzi, Sangallo the Younger, Michelangelo, Vignola, della Porta, Fontana and Carlo Maderna

The 84-foot obelisk that sits in the centre of the square was moved there from an earlier, Roman Empire, site. Transported from the upper Nile and erected in 41AD, this remarkable feat of engineering took six months to complete.

Photographer: Richard Glover/1772:210

St. Peter's, The Vatican, Rome, Italy (1506–1626)

Bramante, Raphael, Peruzzi, Sangallo the Younger, Michelangelo, Vignola, della Porta, Fontana and Carlo Maderna

Initiated by Pope Julius II, as a monumental and appropriate structure to celebrate St. Peter, the dome, designed by Michelangelo, has been an inspiration for those that followed and is often used as a model.

Photographer: (insert) Peter Brown/1772:10, (main) Richard Glover/1772:200

Fontana di Trevi, Rome, Italy (c. 1732–77)

Fernando Fuga (probably)

Inspired by Bernini, these fountains are one of the renowned landmarks of Rome. A mass of classical figures, rocks and wild horses enchant the observer.

Photographer: Richard Glover/1769:50

Maria Della Salute, Venice, Italy (c. 1630–87)

Baldassare Longhena

At the entrance to the Grand Canal, this white Venetian church sits among the red-tiled roofs of Venice. Scrolled buttresses and radiating chapels cascade from the main dome that is carefully balanced by a minor dome.

Photographer: Ian Lambot/412:10

HÔTEL DE VILLE, PARIS, FRANCE (REBUILT 1876)

Ballu and Deperthes

The original building was rebuilt in the early French Renaissance style of steep northern roofs with dormer windows.

Photographer: Richard Glover/7213:10

AZAY-LE-RIDEAU CHÂTEAU, LOIRE, FRANCE (C. 1518–27)

Retaining its medieval appearance in plan and detail, the château's machicolated cornice and corner turrets reflect in the surrounding lake.
Photographer: Colin Dixon/3874:200

Château Chambord, Loire, France (c. 1519–47)

Domenico da Cortona

Based on the plan of a fortified castle, this 400-room château built for François I has a dichotomy of styles, mannerist roofscape and Renaissance walls.

Photographer: Lark Gilmer/1937:90

Chenonceau Château, France (c. 1515–76)

Jean Bullant and others

Originally consisting of a simple square block with corner turrets, it has had a covered five-arch bridge added, with a gallery built on top.

Photographer: John Stuart Miller/3873:60

CHÂTEAU D'ANET, FRANCE (C. 1548-52)

Philibert de l'Orme

Seen as a one of the first successful integrations of the Italian and French Renaissance, Château d'Anet was mostly destroyed during the French Revolution. Only the five-domed chapel and monumental entrance gates remain intact.

Photographer: Lark Gilmer/1940:100

PAVILION RICHELIEU, THE LOUVRE, PARIS FRANCE (C. 1850–57)

Visconti and H. M. Lefuel

Once the largest royal palace complex in the world, the Louvre is now a world-famous museum. The Pavilion Richelieu, was named after the cardinal who, with Louis XIII, enlarged the original scheme. It is seen here through the modern glass pyramid entranceway to the museum

Photographer: Stephane Couturier/443:30

Napoleon's Arch, The Louvre, Paris, France (c. 1860–65)

H. M. Lefuel

Part of a later adaptation, the archway forms the entrance gateway into the Place du Carrousel, and into the modern glass extension.

Photographer: John Edward Linden/443:280

THE SORBONNE, PARIS, FRANCE (1622–1883)

Jacques Le Mercier, Nenot

After Cardinal Richelieu and Jacques Le Mercier rebuilt The Sorbonne, it was rebuilt again in 1883, to provide more room for the increasing demands of students. It includes an amphitheatre, test rooms, labs, a library with over two million works and an observatory.

Photographer: Richard Glover/7210:10

THE MADELAINE, PARIS, FRANCE (C. 1806–42)

Vignon

Technically an imitation of an octastyle peripteral Roman temple (a porticoed eight-column fronted, columned building) the Madelaine relies heavily on its island site and 23 foot podiumto create its imposing façade

Photographer: Richard Glover/7215:10

Hardwick Hall, Derbyshire, England (c. 1576–97)

Robert Smythson

Famous for its large mullioned and transom windows, Hardwick Hall has an unusual plan of a rectangular block with projecting bays. This is to give the façades a sense of three dimensions, continually playing on light and shade.

Photographer: Richard Bryant/40

ES
ES

BLICKLING HALL, NORFOLK, ENGLAND (1627)

Robert Lyminge

This is a good example of a Jacobean house with domed corner towers and a three-gabled elevation articulated by oriel windows in rose-red brick.

Photographer: Clay Perry/507:360

St. Bride's, London, England (c. 1680, steeple 1701)
Sir Christopher Wren
One of the many London churches of Wren, St Bride's is at the heart of the city. The steeple was added after the church was completed.
Photographer: Lucinda Lambton/1497:30

St. Bride's, London, England (c. 1680, steeple 1701)

Sir Christopher Wren

Detail of the telescopic steeple — the tallest designed by Wren — which appears awkward with the absence of inverted consoles for the series of column stages.

Photographer: Lucinda Lambton/1497:10

HONINGTON HALL, WARWICKSHIRE, ENGLAND (1680)

Sir Christopher Wren (ascribed to)

This elegant building demonstrates the application of Renaissance motifs to a variety of elements — staircases, chimneypieces, panelling and ceilings.

Photographer: Clay Perry/2531:30

BLENHEIM PALACE, OXFORDSHIRE, ENGLAND (C. 1705)

Sir John Vanbrugh

One of the most monumental mansions in England, Blenheim's plan is designed on axial lines with symmetry the intention over all else. Within the central block, with its four-angle turrets, is the great hall — 70 feet long by 45 feet wide and 67 feet high.

Photographer: Ken Kirkwood/1471:50

BLENHEIM PALACE, OXFORDSHIRE, ENGLAND (C. 1705)

Sir John Vanbrugh

Set in formal Italian gardens, Blenheim is Sir John Vanbrugh's masterpiece and one of the last examples of Baroque in England.

Photographer: Ken Kirkwood/1471:90

St. Paul's Cathedral, London, England (c. 1675–1710)

Sir Christopher Wren

Wren's masterpiece replaced the medieval church that had been destroyed in the Great Fire of 1666. The cathedral has 11 listed views around London that can not be obscured by new buildings.

Photographer: Christine Ottewell/8982:70

St. Paul's Cathedral, London, England (c. 1675–1710)

Sir Christopher Wren

The famous double dome of St Paul's is actually based more on Bramante's Tempietto in Rome, than that of St. Peter's.

Photographer: Richard Waite/825:70

ST. PAUL'S CATHEDRAL, LONDON, ENGLAND (C. 1675–1710)

Sir Christopher Wren

The dome of St. Paul's is constructed in three parts; the outer dome, which is solely decorative, the inner brick cone which takes the weight of the lantern and cross, and the shallow inner dome only visible from the inside.

Photographer: David Churchill/825:270

Hampton Court Palace, Surrey, England (c. 1689–95)

Sir Christopher Wren

From Wren's extensive extension plans to rebuild Hampton Court, only the south wing and the Fountain Court were realised. As with many of Wren's domestic works, he employed brickwork with stone dressings.

Photographer: David Churchill/1005:390

CHISWICK HOUSE, LONDON, ENGLAND (C. 1725)

Lord Burlington and William Kent

With the help of William Kent, Lord Burlington built on the outskirts of London a similar villa to Palladio's Villa Rotunda. Dispensing with the symmetrical staircases, Burlington opted for a more Baroque pair on the front façade.

Photographer: Clay Perry/1486:50

RADCLIFFE CAMERA, OXFORD UNIVERSITY, OXFORDSHIRE, ENGLAND (C. 1737–48)

James Gibbs

The library at Oxford was inspired and based on Bramante's Tempietto. The Radcliffe Camera, (100 feet in diameter) is Gibbs' most monumental building.

Photographer: Peter Brown/4990:100

THE CIRCUS, BATH, AVON, ENGLAND (C. 1754)

John Wood the Younger

Emphasising the Roman origins of Bath and in the tradition of his father, John Wood the Younger created a series of town houses based around a central garden.

Photographer: Natalie Tepper/2382:50

Assembly Rooms
Costume Museum
Carriage Museum

KEDLESTON HALL, ENGLAND (C. 1759)

Robert Adam

The hall has the appearance of an ancient basilica with its 25-foot high alabaster colonnades of Corinthian columns, surmounted by a covered ceiling. This is the most impressive apartment in the mansion as the space soars its entire height.

Photographer: Richard Bryant/93:180

Stowe Gardens, Buckinghamshire, England (1697, altered 1775)

Robert Adam, Sir John Vanbrugh and others

Famed equally for the garden by Capability Brown, Vanbrugh's houses and temples display simplicity and a pure sensibility.

Photographer: David Fowler/1465:310

Fitzroy Square (East Side), London, England (c. 1790)

Robert Adam

Town planning became a big issue in the late 18th century. Robert Adam — like his contemporaries, notably the Woods in Bath — designed unifying street façades keeping to the same building line.

Photographer: Clay Perry/2520:10

CASTLE HOWARD, YORKSHIRE, ENGLAND (C. 1702–14)

Sir John Vanbrugh with Nicholas Hawksmoor

Displaying the swashbuckling past of Vanbrurgh — once arrested in France for being a spy — the interiors of Castle Howard create a drama of light, which arrives via the central dome.

Photographer: Lucinda Lambton/956:210

CASTLE HOWARD, YORKSHIRE, ENGLAND (C. 1702–14)

Sir John Vanbrugh with Nicholas Hawksmoor

One of the masterpieces of English Baroque, Castle Howard was Vanbrugh's first commission. The ornate dome raised on a high drum dominates the view from all sides even after being substantially rebuilt following a fire in 1940.

Photographer: Clay Perry/956:70

Cumberland Terrace, Regents Park, London, England (c. 1826–27)

John Nash

The neo-Classical terraces of London's Regents Park are translations of the country estates, creating continuous frontages. Articulated by giant Ionic pilasters and projecting porticoes, the three large blocks are linked by triumphal arches.

Photographer: Richard Waite/627:200

ROYAL NAVAL COLLEGE, GREENWICH, LONDON, ENGLAND (C. 1696-1702)

Sir Christopher Wren

One of the great sights of London — the former hospital sits dramatically on the banks of the River Thames. Framing the modest Palladian Queen's House by Inigo Jones, Wren's Royal Naval College features twin towers on coupled colonnades.

Photographer: Alex Bartel/1613:60

SOANE MUSEUM, LONDON, ENGLAND (C. 1813)

Sir John Soane

The breakfast room of Soane's former home — a personal interpretation of classical taste — demonstrates his fascination with the play of light on a space. Lowered ceilings and reflections in glass were all used to create a sense of space in the limited area available.

Photographer: Richard Bryant/521:530

THE ALCAZAR, SEGOVIA, SPAIN (C. 1352–1583)

The view is dominated by the old Catalonian Castillion castle with its massive towers and later Gothic additions.
Photographer: Joe Cornish/9132:10

THE ALCAZAR, SEGOVIA, SPAIN (C. 1352–1583)

Set on a hill in the Catalan region of north Spain, The Alcazar commands the rural landscape — as was the intention of its founders.

Photographer: Mark Fiennes/995:20

THE CATHEDRAL, THE CITADEL VICTORIA (RABAT), GOZO, MALTA (C. 1711)

Within a fortified town, the cathedral shows the translation of the Renaissance style in the Mediterranean.

Photographer: Natalie Tepper/7307:20

Crown Pavilion, The Zwinger, Dresden, Germany (c. 1732)

Matthaus Daniel Poppelmann

The Rococo palace of The Zwinger is fronted by a large outer court laid out as a French garden.This Baroque masterpiece, commissioned by Augustus II the Strong, Elector of Saxony and King of Poland, was designed as an open-air banqueting hall.

Photographer: Nic Barlow/5344:100

Wall Pavilion, The Zwinger, Dresden, Germany (c. 1732)

Matthaus Daniel Poppelmann

One of the most elaborate of the seven linked pavilions of The Zwinger is the Walled Pavilion with its satyr sculptures,
— originally designed to protect the exotic plants through the winter.

Photographer: Nic Barlow/5344:150

CHURCH AT CARAVACA, SPAIN (C. 1722)

The Baroque style took a hold in Spain as it had done in Italy and Germany. Applying Baroque detailing altered many structures as with this church at Caravaca.

Photographer: Kurwenal/Prisma/4344:10

St. John Nepomuk, Munich, Germany (c. 1733–1746)

Egid Quirin Asam

The extremes of any style are often overwhelming, but in the Baroque, especially the interiors, the ornamentation completely drowns the form of the building.

Photographer: John Edward Linden/5219:10

CHARLOTTENBURG PALACE, BERLIN, GERMANY (C. 1701)

Built by Frederick I of Prussia for his wife Sophie Charlotte, the Charlottenburg was the first garden in Germany laid out in the French Baroque style — the building itself is a mixture of styles. The golden figure that crowns the main dome portrays the Goddess of Fortune.

Photographer: Nic Barlow/5338:10

Schloss Sans Souci, Potsdam, Germany (c. 1763)

Georg von Knobelsdorff

Originally a summerhouse for Frederick II, today it contains one of Europe's best pleasure gardens. The Schloss was constructed to celebrate Frederick II's victory in the Seven Years' War.

Photographer: Nic Barlow/5372:80

Schloss Augustusburg, Brühl, Germany (c. 1748–50)

Johann Conrad Schlaun, François Cuvillies, Balthasar Neumann

The western wing of the palace had state rooms and a main staircase added a quarter of a century later; the staircase was decorated lavishly in the Baroque manner.

Photographer: Nic Barlow/5342:30

ARENYS DE MAR, CATALONIA, SPAIN (18TH CENTURY)

Spanish churches are veritable museums of treasures of art. This screen demonstrates the application of the Baroque style, and even on a small scale exudes overwhelming power.

Photographer: Kurwenal/Prisma/4348:10

CHURCH, DÜRNSTEIN, AUSTRIA (C. 1708)

The Baroque is the style of Catholic countries, typifying the rejuvenation produced by the Counter-Reformation. The use of colour on the exteriors is possibly similar to the way the Greeks had applied it.

Photographer: Natalie Tepper/5566:10

CHURCH, DÜRNSTEIN, AUSTRIA (C. 1708)

The Baroque was the ideal decorative form for Catholic symbolism; it uses powerful heavenly imagery to emphasise the magnificence and omnipotence of the Almighty.

Photographer: Natalie Tepper/5566:4

MELK MONASTERY, MELK, AUSTRIA (C. 1702–14)

Jacob Prandtauer

The exuberance in Baroque and Rococo styles is best seen in the detailing and the bold use of colour.

Photographer: Natalie Tepper/5565:90

MELK MONASTERY, MELK, AUSTRIA (C. 1702–14)

Jacob Prandtauer

Built on a bluff above the Danube, the twin towers of the façade with their angled onion domes eclipse the surrounding red-tiled roofs.

Photographer: Natalie Tepper/5565:10

St. Florian Monastery, Linz, Austria (18th century)

Eminently suited to interior decoration; recurring decorative motifs both in the painting and in the stuccowork are the predominant features of Baroque. The curves in this style are more a form of decoration than any technical necessity.

Photographer: Natalie Tepper/5561:100

GROTTO, HELLBRUNN, SALZBURG, AUSTRIA (C. 1617–1750)

Santino Solari

After designing Salzburg Cathedral, Solari was commissioned by Marcus Sitticus, Prince-Archbishop of Salzburg to design his palace and the surrounding landscape. The gardens, which have remained intact, are based on water gardens in Italy.

Photographer: Nic Barlow/5414:150

THE MOSQUE, SCHWETZINGEN, GERMANY (C. 1780)

Nicolas de Pigage

The Mosque is one of many admired follies within the park and an inspiration for many, including Mozart as a child. Reputably costing 120,000 gulden, the Mosque was Elector Carl Theodor's greatest achievement.

Photographer: Nic Barlow/5412:230

THE NEUE SCHLOSS/ERMITAGE, BAYREUTH, GERMANY (C. 1735)

Margravine Wilhelmine of Brandenburg-Bayreuth

Two new short curved wings of the old palace frame the temple whose exterior is encrusted with pebbles and glass.

Photographer: Nic Barlow/5336:20

The Russian Church, Bad Homburg Spa Park, Germany (c. 1841)

Bad Homburg was established as the first European spa with a casino, and was famed as the location where Edward VII created the Homburg hat.

Photographer: Nic Barlow/5334:40

THAI PAVILION, BAD HOMBURG SPA PARK, GERMANY (C. 1841)

The Thai Pavilion displays the elaborate detailing of oriental architecture and the similar principles of application in the Baroque.
Photographer: Nic Barlow/5334:30

THE ORANGERY, WEIKERSDORF, BADEN, AUSTRIA (C. 1866)

Now primarily used for concerts, Baden has always had close links to music — it was here that Mozart composed *Ave Verum*, while Beethoven felt so inspired that he spent 15 summers here composing.

Photographer: Nic Barlow/5333:10

Santa Maria Della Assunta, Venice, Italy (11th century)

The interior of the 11th century church has been transformed with the application of Baroque styling.
Photographer: Ian Lambot/393:10

Lyceum Theatre, London, England (mid-19th century, refurbishment 1997)

Detail of the shell-like decorative motif — a principle characteristic feature of the Rococo style.
Photographer: David Churchill/8071:20

Lyceum Theatre, London, England (mid-19th century, refurbishment 1997)

The Rococo interior decorations of this famous London theatre have recently been refurbished back to its original opulence.
Photographer: David Churchill/8071:50

GALLERIA VITTORIO EMMANUELLE, MILAN, ITALY (C. 1863–67)

Giuseppe Mengoni

Still one of the best examples of roofed pedestrian streets, the Galleria Vittorio Emmanuelle is expressive of the freedom iron gave to overcome structural difficulties.

Photographer: Richard Bryant/2233:50

Galleria Vittorio Emmanuelle, Milan, Italy (c. 1863–67)

Giuseppe Mengoni

An octagon of 128 feet in diameter, rising 96 feet in height, is the centre hub for the cruciform plan.

Photographer: Richard Bryant/2233:80

ARC DE TRIOMPHE, PARIS, FRANCE (C. 1806)

Jean François Therese Chalgrin

Remaining faithful to the Classical style, Chalgrin's Arc de Triomphe is a landmark in Paris sitting at the hub of 12 roads — the main being the world-famous Champs-Elysées.

Photographer: Alex Bartel/3128:10

ARC DE TRIOMPHE, PARIS, FRANCE (C. 1806)

Jean François Therese Chalgrin

Decorative elements are minimal in comparison to other triumphal arches around the world; however, large-scale sculptures adorn the façades on the bases of the columns.

Photographer: Richard Glover/3128:40

Arc de Triomphe, Paris, France (c. 1806)

Jean François Therese Chalgrin

Seen at night, this masterpiece by Chalgrin — a building he did live to see completed — is in the Boulée style of Romantic Classicism.

Photographer: Alex Bartel/3128:20

Sacré-Cœur, Paris, France (c. 1875)

Paul Abadie

Undertaken after the Franco-Prussian War, the eclectic church is one of the major landmarks of Paris, standing on the heights of Montmarte where its white façade glitters in the sunlight.

Photographer: David Churchill/2338:40

Sacré-Cœur, Paris, France (c. 1875)

Paul Abadie

A cluster of white domes with a Byzantine quality about it, the Sacré-Coeur's interiors are richly decorated with fine details.

Photographer: David Churchill/2338:50

EIFFEL TOWER, PARIS, FRANCE (C. 1887–89)

Gustav Eiffel

Some cities have cathedrals, others have civic buildings, and Paris has the Eiffel Tower as its icon. Built for the Paris Exhibition of 1889, it remains a monumental example of frame building.

Photographer: John Edward Linden/5205

Gare Du Nord, Paris, France (c. 1861–65 AD)

Léonce Reynaud

The north station of Paris was built to express the power and monumentality of the railway system, using Classical elements and motifs.

Photographer: Alex Bartel/5083:10

NORD
NORD

L'Opéra, Paris, France (c. 1861–75)

Charles Garnier

This bold Neo-Baroque building was designed in an attempt to create a Napoleon III style; sculptures decorate the colonnaded façade.

Photographer: Colin Dixon/3127:70

L'Opéra, Paris, France (c. 1861–1875)

Charles Garnier

The Opera's sumptuousness is carried through to the interiors, sculptures grace the long foyer and grand staircase both inside and out.

Photographer: Colin Dixon/3127:90

BRIGHTON PAVILION, BRIGHTON, EAST SUSSEX, ENGLAND (C. 1815–1821)

John Nash

A small house originally, remodelled by Nash for the Prince Regent (later George IV) in pseudo Indo-Chinese style. Onion domes and minarets were used extensively throughout — a truly bizarre building but a firm favourite with many.

Photographer: David Churchill/3448

Buckingham Palace, London, England (c. 1825)

John Nash

The London home of the Queen, architecturally Buckingham Palace is at most a competent building, it adds little to the glorious patchwork of the city.

Photographer: Justin Paul/1799:70

BANK OF ENGLAND, CITY OF LONDON, ENGLAND (C. 1732–1937)

George Sampson, Sir John Soane, Herbert Baker, Sir Arthur Blomfield

The Bank of England is the central bank of the United Kingdom, sometimes known as the "Old Lady of Threadneedle Street". It stands, literally and figuratively, at the financial centre of the City of London. Classical Orders of Corinthian columns at the Bank of England, were still seen as representative of authority and power.

Photographer: Richard Bryant/1017:60

BANK OF ENGLAND, CITY OF LONDON, ENGLAND (C. 1732–1937)

George Sampson, Sir John Soane, Herbert Baker, Sir Arthur Blomfield

The Bank of England was founded in 1694 to assist financing the war William III was waging in the Low Countries. It developed into becoming the nation's bank, and managing the national debt.

Photographer: Alex Bartel/1017:110

Houses of Parliament, London, England (c. 1836–51)

Sir Charles Barry and A. W. N. Pugin

The clock tower of the Parliament with its famous bell, Big Ben, makes the building a much-loved audible feature of London as well as a visual one.

Photographer: Alex Bartel/650:510

Houses of Parliament, London, England (c. 1836–51)

Sir Charles Barry and A. W. N. Pugin

Barry was the main architect, but the elevations were the work of Pugin, due to the government wishing to have a Gothic design; Barry had enlisted Pugin as the leading contemporary authority on Gothic.

Photographer: Mark Fiennes/650:60

HOUSES OF PARLIAMENT, LONDON, ENGLAND (C. 1836–51)

Sir Charles Barry and A. W. N. Pugin

The Houses of Parliament are one of the features of the London skyline recognised instantly around the world. They are seen here across Westminster Bridge from the south bank of the River Thames.

Photographer: Richard Bryant/650:70

St. Pancras Station and Hotel, London, England (c. 1865)

Sir George Gilbert Scott

The introduction of trains brought about the need for large terminus stations to bring people in and out of London. Although the station frontage and hotel are Scott's Gothic style, the great train shed at the rear was deigned by W.H. Barlow.

Photographer: Mark Fiennes/1413:210

THE ROYAL COURTS OF JUSTICE, LONDON ENGLAND (C. 1874–1882)

G. E. Street

Designed on an awkward site The Royal Courts of Justice were G.E. Streets greatest achievement and one of the last attempts at Gothic Revival in Britain.

Photographer: Nicholas Kane/2462:60

THE FOUNDER'S BUILDING, ROYAL HOLLOWAY COLLEGE, EGHAM, SURREY, ENGLAND (C. 1879)

W. H. Crossland

The centrepiece of the college is the magnificent and ornate Founder's Building. The beauty of the college lies in its magnificent architecture amongst the splendours of its rural campus.

Photographer: Dennis Gilbert/4412:20

Adobe Houses, Taos Pueblo, New Mexico, United States (19th century)

Modern interpretation of traditional settlements of the indigenous Indians of North America.
Photographer: Farrel Grehan/4637:20

BILTMORE HOUSE, ASHEVILLE, NORTH CAROLINA, UNITED STATES (C. 1888–95)

Richard Morris Hunt

Biltmore was based on the chateaux of the Loire and designed for the wealthy industrialist George Washington Vanderbilt. In contrast to the largely unadorned rear elevation overlooking open country, the front elevation has rich ornamentation creating a formal entrance.

Photographer: Mark Fiennes/1341:10

THE CAPITOL, WASHINGTON D.C., UNITED STATES (1793–1867)

William Thornton, Benjamin Latrobe and Walter Ustick Walter

A symbol of economic power not only in the United States, but also of the Western world, the Capitol building — though based on the Parthenon's basic shape — incorporates iron in the dome.

Photographer: Alex Bartel/3133:80

Labrah and Pebble Hill, Thomasville, Georgia, United States (1842–1935)

Abraham Garfield

A Greek Revival town in Georgia, the main houses date from the middle of the 19th century. Pebble Hill was rebuilt in the early part of the 20th century.

Photographer: Mark Fiennes/1359:30

HAMILTON TWOMBLY HOUSE, MADISON, NEW JERSEY, UNITED STATES (C. 1890–1900)

McKim, Mead, and White

Strongly influenced by Wren, but not in the sense of proportion and shape, Twombly (who had married into the Vanderbilts) wanted a house of an English country gentleman.

Photographer: Mark Fiennes/1364:10

WHITEHALL (FLAGER MANSION), PALM BEACH, WEST PALM BEACH, FLORIDA, UNITED STATES (C. 1903)

Carrere & Hastings Architects

Originally intended as a Spanish palace, Henry M. Flager instructed his architects that he preferred the Colonial style. In its heyday Whitehall became fashionable as the centre for rich Americans during the war in Europe.

Photographer: Mark Fiennes/1343:10

Plum Orchard, Cumberland Island, Georgia, United States (c. 1898)

Peabody and Stearns

The Plum Orchard owned by Thomas Carnegie was the largest and grandest house on an old plantation site, boasting its own swimming pool and squash court, generating plant, laundry, barn, water tower and chicken house.

Photographer: Mark Fiennes/1350:70

WHEATLEIGH, LENOX, MASS., UNITED STATES (C. 1892)

Peabody and Stearns

Built as a wedding present for Count Carlos de Hereida from his father-in-law H. R. Cook (a descendant of Captain Thomas Cook), Wheatleigh is a colonnaded yellow-brick Italiante villa.

Photographer: Mark Fiennes/1337:10

PLANTING FIELDS, LONG ISLAND, NEW YORK, (C. 1900)

A thoroughly English conventional country house in the Tudor style — rather surprising since the owner, William Robertson Coe,went on to purchase Buffalo Bill's house in Wyoming.

Photographer: Mark Fiennes/1354:10

Palace of Fine Arts, San Francisco, California, United States (c. 1915)

Bernard Maybeck

The Palace of Fine Arts is in an exotic and effervescent style of the Bat Region, a West Coast adaptation of Classicism.

Photographer: John Edward Linden/7446:20

CAUMSETT HOUSE, LONG ISLAND, NEW YORK, UNITED STATES (1921)

John Russell Pope

The house, part of a 2,000-acre estate overlooking the Long Island Sound, was the home of Marshall Field III, grandson of the founder of the famous Chicago store. Its design was modelled after Belton House in Lincolnshire.

Photographer: Mark Fiennes/1332:20

Lincoln Memorial, Washington D.C., United States (c. 1922)

Henry Bacon

A white Corinthian monument immortalised on the back of the US penny, Bacon's Lincoln Memorial falls firmly into the Beaux-Art Classical tradition. The architect was a graduate from the office of McKim, Mead, and White.

Photographer: John Edward Linden/7525:10

TENNESSEE
OHIO
LOUISIANA
INDIANA
MISSISSIPPI
ILLINOIS
ALABAMA
MAINE
MISSOURI
CALIFORNIA

MYANMAR PAGAN, BURMA (13TH CENTURY)

The religious philosophies of the region are vividly expressed in the exuberant decoration and architecture of this Burmese shrine.
Photographer: Farrel Grehan/4822:20

MYANMAR PAGAN, BURMA (13TH CENTURY)

The spread of organised religion profoundly influenced the traditional architecture of Southeast Asia. Until then these sacred places expressed the region's architectural direction as well as being the focal point of local devotion.

Photographer: Farrel Grehan/4822:30

MYANMAR PAGAN, BURMA (13^{TH}CENTURY)

Like so many early civilizations the first material used for buildings was the local wood, but craftsmen soon turned to stone after it was accepted as a "sacred" material.

Photographer: Farrel Grehan/4822:50

MEI-MEI-AN TEA HOUSE, MATSUE, JAPAN

A distinctly Japanese social institution, teahouses accommodated the tea-drinking ceremony. Built on a small scale, these indigenous structures had great care placed upon them.

Photographer: Bill Tingey/5655:10

HEIAN JINGU GARDEN, KYOTO, JAPAN (8TH–12TH CENTURY)

After the fall of the Tiang dynasty, the first indigenous domestic architecture came in the form of country houses for lords of regional clans. Usually they took the pattern of a series of rectangular buildings connected by corridors.

Photographer: Bill Tingey/5649:130

Heian Jingu Garden, Kyoto, Japan (8th–12th century)

These typical roofs bear a general resemblance to those of China, but as a rule they were simpler in design. Below the main roof the "hisashi", or lower roof, sometimes projected out below the upper eaves.

Photographer: Bill Tingey/5649:120

HIMEJI CASTLE, JAPAN (C.1570)

Multiple roofs in Oriental architecture are commonplace. Himeji Castle — like many castles — has an adventurous roof with gables pointing in all directions. Known as the White Heron, the castle roofs were designed to resemble seabirds ready for flight.

Photographer: Alex Bartel/2953:10

Wat Pho, Bangkok, Thailand (15th century)

Distinctive intricate detailing and local motifs decorate the eaves and gable ends of the roofs within the Asian subcontinent.
Photographer: Richard Glover/2597:40

Temple, Bangkok, Thailand (15th century)

Temples were often fortified as they usually contained riches and treasures, as well as being sacred sites. Variations on the same theme could be seen, although each region has its own style for detailing domes, spires and gable roofs.

Photographer: Peter Brown/1783:10

IMPERIAL PALACE, FORBIDDEN CITY, BEIJING, CHINA (C. 1602)

At the centre of the Forbidden City lies the Imperial Palace consisting of three vast halls — all similar in design.

Photographer: Natalie Tepper/5553:10

MERIDIAN GATE, BEIJING, CHINA (C. 1602)

The Forbidden City is reminiscent of a Chinese Box — a series of gates, bridges and squares have to be negotiated. After passing through Tiananmen Square, access is via the Meridian Gate, then across a horseshoe canal before you reach the series of gate houses, then eventually into the heart of the complex.

Photographer: Natalie Tepper/5552:10

IMPERIAL PALACE, FORBIDDEN CITY, BEIJING, CHINA (C.1602)

A decorative panel from one of the gate house guarding the palace.
Photographer: Natalie Tepper/5553:100

IMPERIAL PALACE, FORBIDDEN CITY, BEIJING, CHINA (C. 1602)

One of the many pavilions that lie within the gardens of the Forbidden City.
Photographer: Natalie Tepper/5553:130

THE DOME OF THE ROCK, JERUSALEM, ISRAEL (688–692 AD)

The parapet wall conceals the shallow pitched roof that surrounds the drum of the dome and allows a continuous decorative vertical surface.
Photographer: Robert O'Dea/3972:170

THE DOME OF THE ROCK, JERUSALEM, ISRAEL (C. 688-692 AD)

Rising above the western wall, the golden cupola of the Dome has been a significant sight for pilgrims to Jerusalem, — whether Jewish, Christian, or Muslim.

Photographer: Richard Bryant/3972:10

NUWEIBA BEACH, THE SINAI, EGYPT

These beach huts — although modern — contain regional iconic imagery replicating the Byzantine domes of their basic shape.
Photographer: Robert O'Dea/8067:30

The Blue Mosque, Istanbul, Turkey (c. 1606–16)

As large as the domes of the mosques are — almost flat in comparison to the Roman domes — the minarets dwarfed them, and were a hallmark of the Ottoman style.

Photographer: Richard Glover/7462:20

THE BLUE MOSQUE, ISTANBUL, TURKEY (C. 1606–16)

The use of multiple domes on the mosques was a trait of the Ottoman Empire, the many important points of the building each had their own dome, but all were subordinate to the large central dome.

Photographer: Richard Glover/7462:50

SULEYMANIYEH MOSQUE, ISTANBUL, TURKEY (C. 1551–58)

Koca Sinan

The main structure resembles that of St. Sophia but on a smaller scale, the dome has a diameter of 86 feet with a height of 156 feet. Internally the walls are lined with coloured marbles, while the "mihrab" is white framed in coloured Persian tiles.

Photographer: Richard Glover/7468:10

Palace of Alhambra (Qalat al-Hamra), Granada, Spain (c.1370–80)

Hidden beneath the dazzling tessellated filigree of the fretting and stalacitie, the palace is a collection of pavilions linked together by elaborate courts.

Photographer: Kurwenal/Prisma/1943:150

PALACE OF ALHAMBRA (QALAT AL-HAMRA), GRANADA, SPAIN (C.1370–80)

The Alhambra is one of the most decorated Islamic palaces anywhere. At the very heart of the complex are the Court of the Lions and the Court of the Myrtle Trees — these lead to the audience chambers of the Moorish rulers.

Photographer: Kurwenal/Prisma/1943:130

Casa De Pilatos, Seville, Spain (15th–16th century)

Antonio Maria Aprile

The main patio is in the Renaissance style, with Mudejar ornamentation. It has a fountain in the middle and two statues representing the goddess Palas in the corners.

Photographer: Richard Bryant/3306:20

CASA DE PILATOS, SEVILLE, SPAIN (15TH–16TH CENTURY)

Antonio Maria Aprile

The façade, by Antonio Maria Aprile in 1529, is clearly Renaissance, but it is crowned by a Gothic cresting, perhaps brought from the Riberas' palace in Bornos.

Photographer: Richard Bryant/3306:50

THE GRANDE HOTEL, TANGIER, MOROCCO (19TH CENTURY)

Using the local vernacular architecture, the Grande Hotel has been used in Bertolucci's *Sheltering Sky* film.
Photographer: Richard Waite/4826:80

THE GRANDE HOTEL, TANGIER, MOROCCO (19TH CENTURY)

Mosaics of tiles adorn the walls and floors — an architectural detail common in Moorish architecture.
Photographer: Richard Waite/4826:10

VILLA MAROC, ESSAOUIRA, MOROCCO (1990)

Located in the town where Orson Welles' filmed his production of *Othello*, the Villa Maroc consists of two Medina houses centred around internal courtyards.

Photographer: Richard Waite/4827:60

KING HASSAN II MOSQUE, CASABLANCA, MOROCCO (1994)

Standing three times larger than St. Paul's and proposed as the Eighth Wonder of the World, King Hussan II was inspired by reading the Koran to build a new mosque.

Photographer: Nick Meers/5140:100

King Hassan II Mosque, Casablanca, Morocco (1994)

Visible from 30 miles away, plans are in place to beam a laser from the top of the 700-foot minaret for 25 miles in the direction of Mecca.

Photographer: Nick Meers/5140:30

King Hassan II Mosque, Casablanca, Morocco (1994)

The estimated cost of £400 million for the mosque is a fraction of the reputed £5 billion it would have taken to build a bridge between Morocco and Europe as King Hassan had planned in the mid-1980s.

Photographer: Nick Meers/5140:140

HOTEL LA MAMOUNIA, MOROCCO (20TH CENTURY)

A recently renovated hotel, it is famed for the clientele that have stayed including John Lennon, and Winston Churchill who came to Morocco to paint.

Photographer: Julie Phipps/789:70

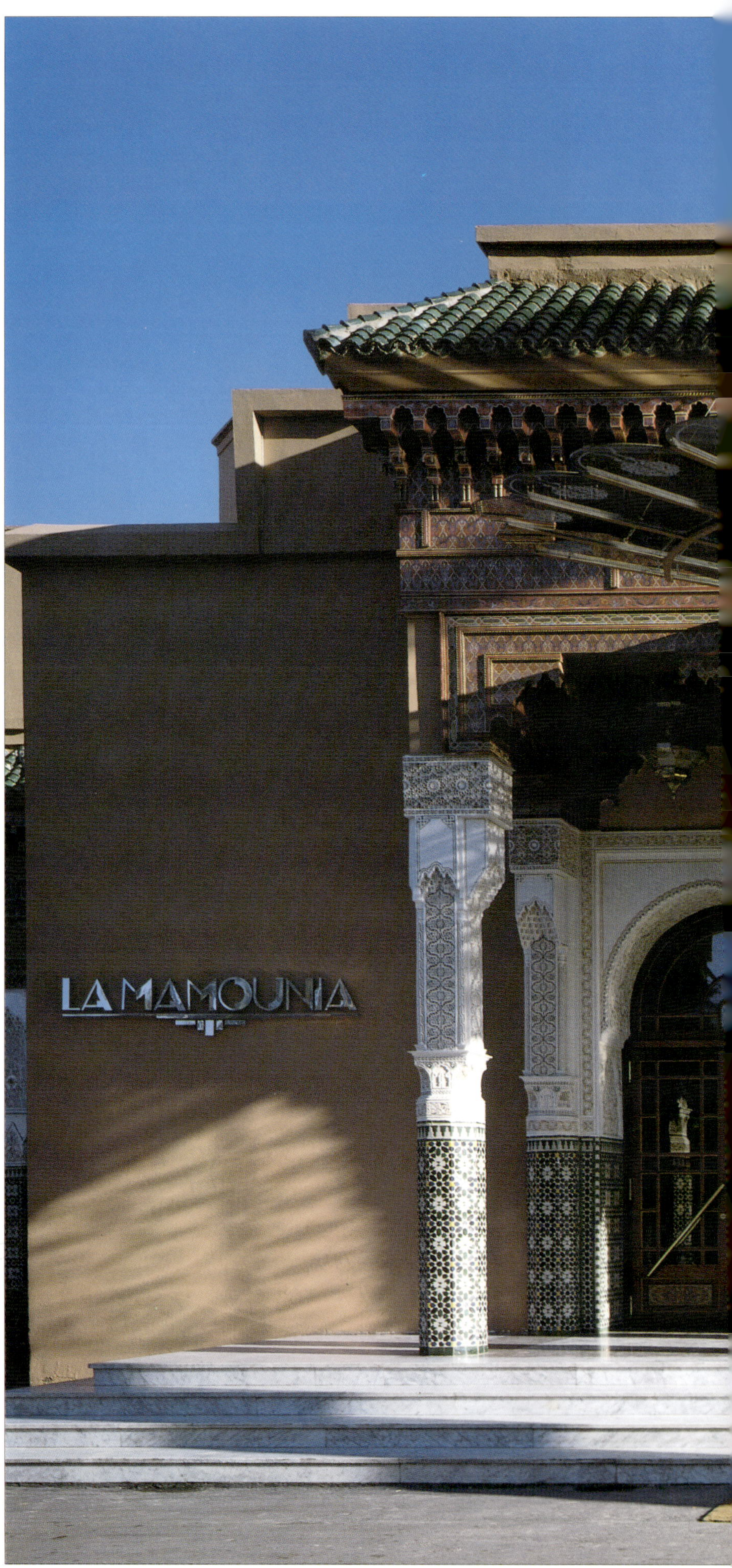

HOTEL LA MAMOUNIA, MOROCCO (20TH CENTURY)

A modern interpretation of the traditional Moorish style, it is an established tenet that Islamic countries stick rigidly to non-figurative vernacular architecture.

Photographer: Julie Phipps/789:20

Sas-Bahu Temple, Udaipur, India (11th century)

A series of towers with a multiplicity of delicate carvings are all that remains of this ancient temple which stands next to another 11th century temple.

Photographer: Peter Brown/1778:20

TEMPLE, DELHI, INDIA (19TH CENTURY)

Rich colours and well-crafted details epitomise much about the craftsmanship of Indian architecture; symbolism is ubiquitous in religious cultures throughout Asia.

Photographer: Peter Brown/1778:10

MAHARAJAS JODHPUR FORT, INDIA (19TH CENTURY)

The fort displays all the elements of Indian architecture, mosaic tiling, patterned rugs, moulded apertures and religious motifs.

Photographer: Peter Brown/1781:10

Taj Mahal, Agar, India (c. 1630–53)

Ali Mardan Khan

Shah Jehan erected this fabulous royal mausoleum for his favourite wife, Mumtaz-I-Mahal. The white marble central dome is nearly 80 feet high with a diameter of 58 feet and is surrounded by 133-foot minarets.

Photographer: Justin Paul/1782:20

THE LAW COURTS, MADRAS, INDIA (19TH CENTURY)

The Law Courts of Madras, with traditional minarets, towers and central dome, conform to the principle elements common to architecture of the region.

Photographer: Alex Bartel/5842:10

Vienna Secessionist, Friedrichstrasse Exhibition Hall, Vienna, Austria (c. 1897–98)

Joseph Maria Olbrich

Abandoning the typical classical ornamentation, Olbrich has used tree forms on the façades. In plan and overall arrangement there is very little difference to the customary exhibition halls.

Photographer: Gisela Erlacher/5112:10

DER·ZEIT·IHRE·KVNST·
DER·KVNST·IHRE·FREIHEIT·

WIGHTWICK MANOR, WOLVERHAMPTON, ENGLAND (C. 1898)

Edward Ould

The original manor house with stables and outbuildings still remains on the site that the Wightwick family had left in 1658. Constructed in two parts, the additions illustrate a more ambitious picturesque vernacular.

Photographer: Richard Bryant/193:40

VICTOR HORTA HOUSE MUSEUM, BRUSSELS, BELGIUM (C. 1900)

Victor Horta

Exploring the potential of iron and stone, Horta creates delicate balustrades, railings and columns. Horta's style can be seen in every element and detail right through to the design of the furniture.

Photographer: Richard Bryant/3363

LITTLE THAKEHAM, WEST SUSSEX, ENGLAND (C. 1900)

Sir Edwin Landseer Lutyens

Viewed as one of the greatest architects of his time, Lutyens changed the face of English country houses in his arrangement of the plan. Building on intuition, his planning of spaces was laid out to be surprising and revealing.

Photographer: Richard Bryant/26:200

FULLER BUILDING, NEW YORK CITY, NEW YORK, UNITED STATES (1902)

Daniel Burnham

Due to its unique site the Fuller Building has always been known as "Flat Iron". Burnham followed Louis Sullivan's direction closely to create a structure which is composed on the lines of a classical column.

Photographer: Niall Clutton/9055:50

25B RUE FRANKLIN, PARIS, FRANCE (1903)

Auguste Perret

Perret's first significant building demonstrated the possibilities afforded by the use of the new reinforced concrete — a reinforced concrete frame was used with infill concrete panels decorated in floral Art Nouveau designs.

Photographer: Paul Raftery/8610:10

Casa Batlló, Barcelona, Spain (1904–06)

Antoni Gaudí

Known as the "House of Bones", Casa Batlló sits at the centre of the Barcelona on the spine road of the city. Its façade is contorted and deformed, articulating the individual apartments as well as the overall structure.

Photographer: Paul Raftery/1208:320

HILL HOUSE, HENSBURGH, SCOTLAND (1903)

Charles Rennie Mackintosh

Covered in harl (roughcast), Hill House is a modern interpretation of an old Scottish tower house. Mackintosh designed all the details throughout the house from furniture to the light fittings, displaying his unique brand of Art Nouveau.

Photographer: Mark Fiennes/480

SANATORIUM, PURKERSDORF BEI WIEN, AUSTRIA (1904–05)

Josef Hoffmann

Hoffmann's design for the Sanatorium became one of the foremost examples of the Modern Movement, various elements of the exteriors were combined in a single surface serving to emphasise the abstract nature of its volumes.

Photographer: Gisela Erlacher/7258:10

VILLA RUGGEI, PESARO, ITALY (1902–07)
Often merely surface decoration, Art Nouveau was bold and Baroque with its complicated use of sculptured foliage.
Photographer: Martine Hamilton Knight/5718:60

Villa Ruggei, Pesaro, Italy (1902–07)

Close attention was paid when creating decorative frames for doors and windows.

Photographer: Martine Hamilton Knight/5718:90

Glasgow School of Art, Glasgow, Scotland (1898–1909)

Charles Rennie Mackintosh

The jewel in Mackintosh's crown is the western extension of the school. The expressive exterior hides the delicate and complex nature of the interior.

Photographer: Natalie Tepper/7690:580

167
167

Glasgow School of Art, Glasgow, Scotland (1898–1909)

Charles Rennie Mackintosh

The interior of the library was constructed with the same care and attention Mackintosh shows in the smallest of details. A clear understanding of the structure and a careful use of decoration creates a delightful space.

Photographer: Mark Fiennes/7690:330

MAGWORLD
PERIODICALS are not to be removed from this room.
INTERIOR DESIGN
exposure
CREATIVE REVIEW

MICHELIN BUILDING, LONDON, ENGLAND (1911)

F. Espinasse

Originally designed for the French tyre company as a working advertisement, the building stands as good example of Art Nouveau in London. Although now straddled by a maladroit extension, the Michelin still remains a landmark building in West London.

Photographer: Richard Bryant/201:90

MICHELIN
81
D344 XBL

GRAND CENTRAL STATION, NEW YORK CITY, NEW YORK, UNITED STATES (1913)

Warren and Wetmore, Reed and Stern

Celebrated in many movies, the famous concourse of Grand Central Station is currently the architectural focus of New York's rail network.

Photographer: Niall Clutton/9055

TERMINAL
BANANA REPUBLIC

GRAND CENTRAL STATION, NEW YORK CITY, NEW YORK, UNITED STATES (1913)

Warren and Wetmore, Reed and Stern

Measuring 119.7ft by 411.7ft by 124.6ft high, the main concourse bathes the passengers in streams of sunlight from the lunettes on high. It has recently undergone a spectacular refurbishment

Photographer: Niall Clutton/9055

Helsinki Station, Helsinki, Finland (1914)

Eliel Saarinen

The giant Nordic torso lamps that light the main entrance to the station are sculpted in granite, and complement the monumental architecture of the façade. The station soon became influential in America whence Saarinen emigrated in 1923.

Photographer: Alex Bartel/2965:10

EINSTEIN TOWER, POTSDAM, GERMANY (1921)

Erich Mendelsohn

Designed to test Albert Einstein's theory of relativity, Mendelsohn's unusual approach to architecture, drawing inspiration from beyond the earth captured Einstein's theoretical essence. Construction constraints made it impossible for the whole vision to be explored, using a single material to express the streamlined form.

Photographer: James F. Neal/8068

NÔTRE DAME DE RAINCY, PARIS, FRANCE (1922–23)

Auguste Perret

A magnificent example of the properties and strength of reinforced concrete; the barrel-vaulted nave is supported on 36ft columns, which have a 14-inch diameter. These columns are also used to allow almost completely glazed external walls.

Photographer: Paul Raftery/8609:10

Schroder House, Utrecht, The Netherlands (1924)

Gerrit Rietveld

Arguably the greatest and most inspiring building to come out of the De Stijl group, the Schroder House is a straight transformation of a Mondrian painting into architecture.

Photographer: Richard Bryant/7163:60

Bauhaus, Dessau, Germany (1926)

Walter Gropius

The new home for the Bauhaus exhibited all the aspects to which Walter Gropius, the school's founder-director, aspired.

Photographer: Dennis Gilbert/3887:10

BAUHAUS

Bauhaus, Dessau, Germany (1926)

Walter Gropius

The glass curtain walling between concrete slabs still symbolises not only the Bauhaus but also the International Movement.

Photographer: Dennis Gilbert/3887:60

SELFRIDGE'S DEPARTMENT STORE, LONDON, ENGLAND (1926)

Daniel Burnham

Essentially a steel-frame building, the largest of its time in Britain, the exterior is dressed in classical clothes, designed by Francis Swales. As one of London's grandest retail stores, it was a revolution for shoppers both in plan and approach to shopping.

Photographer: Mark Fiennes/2473:50

WEISSENHOFSIEDLUNG, STUTTGART, GERMANY (1927)

Ludwig Mies van der Rohe (masterplanner)

The model for how the Modern Movement could be utilised to plan a functional, low-cost housing project, the Weissenhof Estate brought together many of the leading figureheads under the guidance of Mies. His own housing block was influential in America as well as Europe.

Photographer: Richard Bryant/1325:250

Rue Mallet-Stevens housing, Passy, Paris, France (1927)

Robert Mallet-Stevens

Just as Mondrian influenced the De Stijl group, Cubist architecture took its lead from the works of Georges Braque and Pablo Picasso. Though the façades follows these influences, the plans are traditional in nature.

Photographer: Paul Raftery/4939:50

Lovell House, Los Angeles, California, United States (1929)

Richard Neutra

Using standardised factory components, Neutra created a seminal house on a hillside of Los Angeles that demonstrates a purity and elegance more akin to 1920s' Germany than California. His training and work under such names as Loos, Mendelsohn and Wright are clearly evident.

Photographer: Natalie Tepper/7173:20

Chrysler Building, Manhattan, New York City, New York, United States (1930)

William van Alen

This distinctive masterpiece of high-rise building has been an icon since it was constructed, at which time it was briefly the tallest building in the world (1,048 feet). Stretching the capabilities of the technology of the time, the Chrysler Building's ornamentation remains remarkably fresh.

Photographer: Mark Fiennes/474:90

EMPIRE STATE BUILDING, NEW YORK CITY, NEW YORK, UNITED STATES (1931)

Shreve, Lamb and Harmon

Remaining the tallest building in the world for over 40 years (1,250 feet), the Empire State Building is destined to be an abiding icon of the economic growth of the early 20th Century.

Photographer: Niall Clutton/9055:80

KARL MARX HOF, VIENNA, AUSTRIA (1930)

Karl Ehn

Designed as one of a series of large estates by Ehn in Vienna, Karl Marx Hof is an imposing structure, very suggestive of the Expressionist ideas.

Photographer: Gisela Erlacher/8734:10

VILLA SAVOYE, POISSY, FRANCE (1931)

Le Corbusier and Pierre Jeaneret

A beautiful study of the relationships of inside and outside, and light and shadow, Villa Savoye stands as the epitome of early Le Corbusian theories.

Photographer: David Churchill/7402:190

VILLA SAVOYE, POISSY, FRANCE (1931)

Le Corbusier and Pierre Jeaneret

The distinction between the inside and the outside is uncertain in the external upper deck. Le Corbusier manages to bring nature into the heart of the house, while maintaining a sense of enclosure.

Photographer: Paul Raftery/7402:340

MAISON DE VERRE, PARIS, FRANCE (1932)

Pierre Chareau and Bernard Bijvoet

The façade the house presents is a slender steel frame with infill glass blocks, equally opening and closing the interior to the outside. Maison de Verre to this day is still a most extraordinary house.

Photographer: Michael Halberstadt/8072:10

Church of the Holiest Heart of Our Lord, Prague, Czech Republic (1932)

Josip Plecnik

A variety of styles makes up this church which looks like a tombstone, the unusual appearance owing little to any of the trends of the period.

Photographer: Mark Fiennes/6300:10

Daily Express Building, Fleet Street, London, England (1932)

Ellis Clarke, Ronald Atkinson and Owen Williams

The "Black Lubianka", the nickname given to the black glass-wrapped façade of the *Daily Express* building, exudes all the glamour and mystique of the Art Deco style. The exterior shows no sign of the sheer grandeur of the entrance that greets the visitor.

Photographer: Dennis Glibert/1609:10

ST. OLAF HOUSE, LONDON, ENGLAND (1932)

H. S. Goodhart-Rendal

Displaying all the typical telltale signs of Art Deco, St Olaf House sits proudly by London Bridge.

Photographer: Nick Dawe/3853:110

Penguin Pool, Regent's Park Zoo, London, England (1934)

Berthold Lubetkin and Tecton

Simplicity personified is how best to describe the enclosure, with its sweeping concrete ramps over a pool. Designed in conjunction with the Danish engineer Ove Arup, the newly restored pool is a testament to rational design.

Photographer: Chris Gascoigne/501:40

SOUTH BEACH DISTRICT, MIAMI, FLORIDA, UNITED STATES (1930s)

Typical of the buildings, many of them hotels, that occupy South Beach District, the simple forms of Art Deco are expressed in vivid array of colours.

Photographer: Natalie Tepper/4287:340

De La Warr Pavilion, Bexhill-on-Sea, East Sussex, England (1935)

Erich Mendelsohn and Serge Chermayeff

One of the first truly Modernist buildings in Great Britain, the pavilion turns its back on the road and opens itself to the sea.

Photographer: Richard Bryant/7655:50

De La Warr Pavilion, Bexhill-on-Sea, East Sussex, England (1935)

Erich Mendelsohn and Serge Chermayeff

The centrepiece is an ethereal spiral staircase wrapped in a glass sleeve, overlooking the seemingly endless sea

Photographer: Richard Bryant/7655:50

1930s Car Showroom, on the A30, Egham, Surrey, England (1930s)

The Modern Movement's aesthetics not only became ideal for functions such as petrol stations but were also seen suitable for car showrooms.

Photographer: Nick Dawe/8534:10

Ferrari
Ferrari
MARANELLO SALES LIMITED
L144 BPA
K601 YPD

HIGHPOINT 1, HIGHGATE, LONDON, ENGLAND (1935)

Berthold Lubetkin and Tecton

This concrete housing block, designed so the walls took its own weight, was given a seal of approval by Le Corbusier on a visit to London. Such was the impact the 64-flat block made, that it became home to many figures from the Modern Movement.

Photographer: Yoke Matza/8984

Fallingwater, Bear Run, Pennsylvania, United States (1936)

Frank Lloyd Wright

It is hard to distinguish between nature and the man-made when viewing Wright's domestic *tour de force*. The projecting horizontal planes that dominate the house all work off the central fireplace, a Wright trademark. Fallingwater is one of the best examples of the symbiotic relationship of man and nature.

Photographer: Martin Jones/476:240

CORONET (FORMERLY THE ODEON) CINEMA, WOOLWICH, LONDON, ENGLAND (1937)

George Coufs

In the golden age of cinema, before the advent of television, the cinema held a special place with the public. The structures that housed moving pictures were given unique status and this was reflected in the architecture of the cinemas.

Photographer: Nick Dawe/8509:10

METRO MAYAKOVSKAYA, MOSCOW, RUSSIA (1938)

Aleksei Dushkin

The winner of the Gold Prix at the 1938 New York World Fair, Dushkin's design demonstrates the authoritative Neo-classical forms that kept him in official favour. Soviet motifs, which decorate the arches, are lit by a series of bronze torches and lamps.

Photographer: Alex Bartel/2964:10

Hoover Building, Perivale, London, England (1932–38)

Wallis, Gilbert and Partners

One of the great attractions of west London, the Hoover Factory, though not liked by everyone, is an enigmatic attempt to enliven the workplace. Like other buildings of this time, its function has changed and the purity of the design slightly sullied by the new occupiers.

Photographer: Nick Dawe/350:270

ER BUILDING

ROCKEFELLER CENTER, NEW YORK CITY, NEW YORK, UNITED STATES (1940)

Reinhard and Hofmeister and others

Visitors are greeted at the tower by Art Deco panels above the doorways, before entering the sumptuous lobby space.

Photographer: Richard Bryant/475:50

ROCKEFELLER CENTER, NEW YORK CITY, NEW YORK, UNITED STATES (1940)

Reinhard and Hofmeister and others

A large complex of civic buildings on a 12-acre site in the heart of New York, this Art Deco styled series of buildings spared little in the way of finishes. As much famed for the temporary outdoor ice rink, the Rockefeller is opulent excess personified.

Photographer: Niall Clutton/9055:150

NATIONAL GALLERY OF ART, WASHINGTON D.C., UNITED STATES (1940)

John Russell Pope

As with many East Coast public buildings, Classicism seems to be the style chosen to represent democracy in its purest sense. The National is a competent attempt to recreate the Palladian design.

Photographer: John Edward Linden/360:330

NATIONAL GAL

PALACE OF ITALIAN CIVILISATION, ROME, ITALY (1942)

Guerrini, Lapadula and Romano

Abandoned because of the onset of World War Two, the Expositione Universale Roma architectural centrepieces were built and survive today. The Palace of Italian civilisation dominates the area, sitting uncomfortably on a raised plinth, offering no sense of humanity to on-lookers.

Photographer: Richard Waite/2347:30

Glass House, New Canaan, Connecticut, United States (1950)

Philip Johnson

Created as a retreat for himself, Johnson, the architectural chameleon, displayed a clear understanding of the teachings of the Bauhaus, especially Miesian theory. An unobtrusive house becoming part of the surroundings.

Photographer: Richard Bryant/35:310

Expositione Universale Roma Church,
Rome, Italy (1942)

As with the Palace of Italian Civilisation, this church uses ancient buildings of Rome for inspiration, particularly the Pantheon. However, the *ésprit de corps* of Ancient Rome has been lost in the interpretation.

Photographer: Richard Waite/2347:60

Johnson Wax Building, Racine, Wisconsin, United States (1950)

Frank Lloyd Wright

The open plan offices, with their Wright designed furniture, are overwhelmed by the sheer scale of the mushroom columns that support the top-lit roof.

Photographer: Farrel Grehan/3450:80

Johnson Wax Building, Racine, Wisconsin, United States (1950)

Frank Lloyd Wright

Developed between 1936 and 1950, the Johnson Wax building reflects the growing optimism of America in the post-war years. Two distinct parts of the factory exist, the open plan offices and the laboratory tower with its alternative circular mezzanine floors.

Photographer: Farrel Grehan/3450:90

ROYAL FESTIVAL HALL, SOUTH BANK, LONDON, ENGLAND (1951)

LCC Architects Department

Built for the Festival of Britain in 1951, the Royal Festival Hall is a well thought out solution to the problems of reducing noise. An unsuitable position led to the "egg in a box" design for which the hall is famed.

Photographer: Martin Jones/2103:20

UNITÉ D'HABITATION, MARSEILLES, FRANCE (1952)

Le Corbusier

Of the five *Unités* Le Corbusier designed, Marseilles, the original, still remains the clearest manifestation of his theories of social housing, though it is now mainly occupied by middle class residents. The *Unité* contains shops, gyms, swimming pools and a hotel, Hôtel Le Corbusier.

Photographer: Paul Raftery/7401:100

SAYNATSALO TOWN HALL, SAYNATSALO, FINLAND (1952)

Alvar Aalto

Arguably the most attractive of Aalto's public buildings, the Town Hall proves that modern architecture could realise its ideals, while retaining its humanity and consciousness of the natural surroundings. The small collection of pitched roofed buildings, council chambers, offices, library, shops, a bank and a post office, are grouped around a raised courtyard.

Photographer: Richard Einzig/2419:50

LOMONOSOV STATE UNIVERSITY, MOSCOW, RUSSIA (1953)

Lev Rudnev and others

As symbolic as any building designed and built in the Stalin era, the university dominates the landscape conveying authoritarianism to all around. The 26-storey central tower, topped with a spire and Soviet star, overlooks the River Moskva.

Photographer: Alex Bartel/2963:10

BETH SHOLOM SYNAGOGUE, ELKINS PARK, PENNSYLVANIA, UNITED STATES (1954)

Frank Lloyd Wright

A tent of steel, glass and plastic, evoking associations with Indian wig-wams and reflecting the sky,the Beth Sholom Synagogue rises above a triangular plan.

Photographer: Richard Bryant/7314:10

CHAPEL OF NÔTRE DAME-DU-HAUT, RONCHAMP, FRANCE (1955)

Le Corbusier

Standing on a hill of ancient worship, Ronchamp is Le Corbusier's most unique and unusual building. The form appears to bear little relation to any work produced previously and any after. The whole structure and plan of Ronchamp deceives, but this wasn't an exercise in truth to materials, it was exploration of spirituality and remains a must pilgrimage.

Photographer: Arcaid/7400:100

Annunciation Greek Orthodox Church, Wauwatosa, Wisconsin, United States (1956)

Frank Lloyd Wright

In the latter years of Wright's life, he indulged his fascination with the extravagant and the exotic. Experimentation with new forms and new decoration epitomised his later works.

Photographer: Farrel Grehan/7336:10

SOLOMON R. GUGGENHEIM MUSEUM, NEW YORK CITY, NEW YORK, UNITED STATES (1959)

Frank Lloyd Wright

With total disregard to the art and the visitor, Wright's *pièce de résistance* — more than any other building — symbolises the freedom architects enjoyed in the 20th century.

Photographer: Richard Bryant/7311

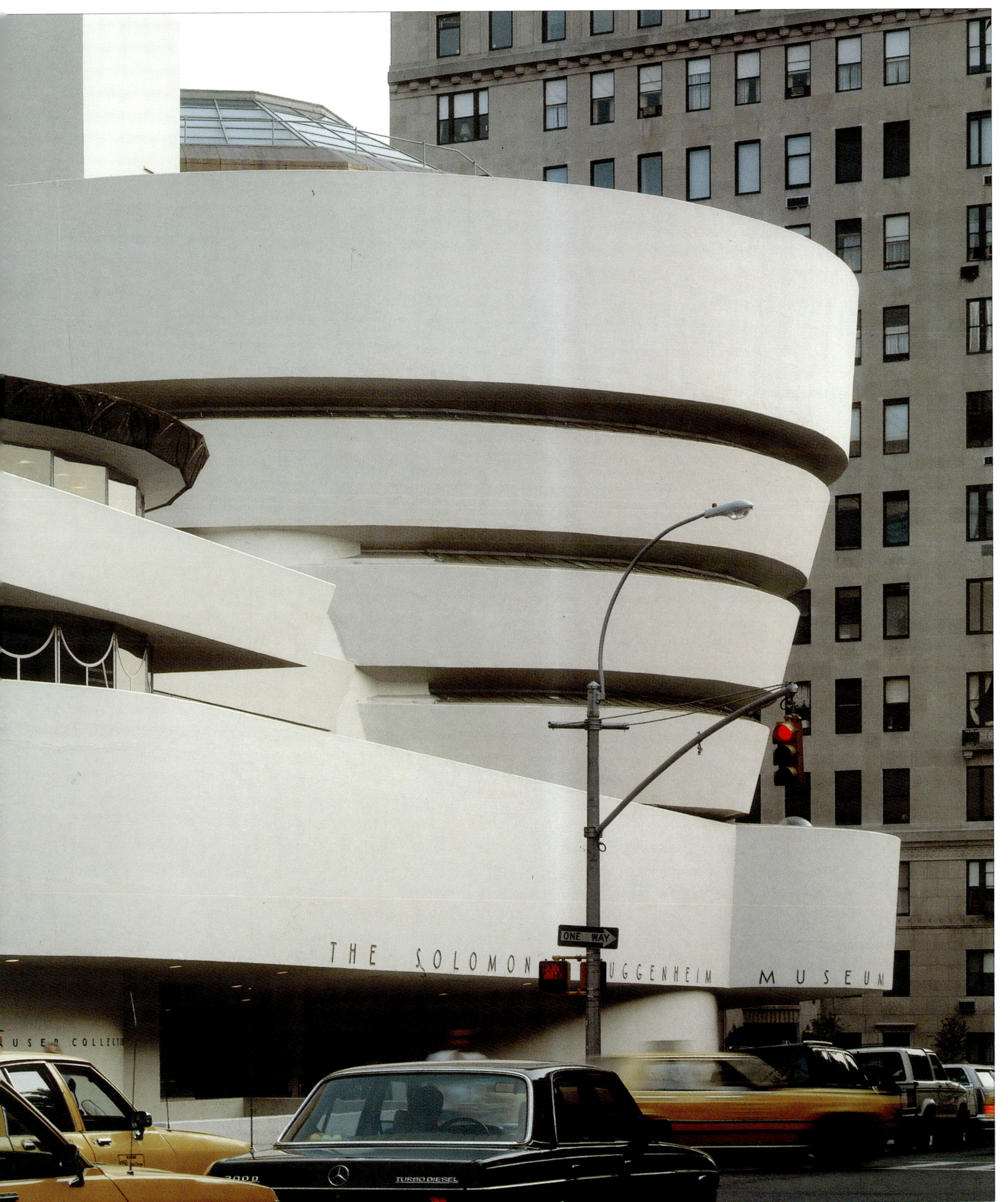
THE SOLOMON
UGGENHEIM
MUSEUM
ONE WAY
TURBO DIESEL

Solomon R. Guggenheim Museum, New York City, New York, United States (1959)

Frank Lloyd Wright

The Guggenheim made an immediate impact and quickly reached icon status. Even 40 years later little matches its boldness.

Photographer: Richard Bryant/7311

Pirelli Tower, Milan, Italy (1959)

Gio Ponti

Breaking away from the tradition Mies had established in building skyscrapers, this tower was constructed with an efficient concrete skeleton allowing for the streamlined appearance.

Photographer: John Croce/4401:10

TORRE VELASCA, MILAN, ITALY (1958)

Belgiojose, Peressutti, and Rogers

As a comment against the blandness of the International style, the top eight floors overhang the remaining tower supported by giant brackets. The scattering of windows further disrupts the formality and smoothness usually found in modern offices.

Photographer: John Croce/5011:20

Congresso Nacional, Brasilia, Brazil (1960)

Oscar Niemeyer

A national competition was held to choose a master plan for Brasilia. The winner was L˙cio Costa, a leader in the modern school of architecture in Brazil. The world-famous Brazilian architect Oscar Niemeyer was chosen to design the public buildings and to approve plans for private construction.

Photographer: Reto Guntli/8922

Congresso Nacional, Brasilia, Brazil (1960)

Oscar Niemeyer

The isolation from the surrounding shantytowns and the intensity of the climate gives sculptural forms a surreal edge; this is Modernism at its most extreme.

Photographer: Reto Guntli/8922

Congresso Nacional, Brasilia, Brazil (1960)

Oscar Niemeyer

The vastness of the masterplan and the scale of Niemeyer's forms render Brasilica's political heart cold and desolate.

Photographer: Reto Guntli/8922

CATEDRAL METROPOLITANA, BRASILIA, BRAZIL (1960)

Oscar Niemeyer

The Catedral Metropolitana is one of several buildings designed by Brazilian architect Oscar Niemeyer in the 1960s for the Brazilian capital, Brasilia. The mostly underground cathedral has 16 curved columns and a stained glass interior.

Photographer: Reto Guntli/8922

TWA Terminal, Idlewild (now JFK) Airport, New York City, New York, United States (1961)

Eero Saarinen

The terminal wings lift to reveal fully glazed ends that allow passengers to wonder at the aeroplanes arriving and departing.

Photographer: Mark Fiennes/3920

TWA Terminal, Idlewild (now JFK) Airport, New York City, New York, United States (1961)

Eero Saarinen

The swooping wings and gentle curves of the TWA Terminal exude confidence not only in the properties of reinforced concrete but the whole principle of flight.

Photographer: Mark Fiennes/3920

PHILHARMONIE AND KAMMER MUSIKSAAL, BERLIN, GERMANY (1963)

Hans Scharoun

Conceived as a huge valley, at the bottom of which sat the orchestra, while at the sides were placed the seats, the magnificent cavern for musical performances is enhanced by the tent-like structure of the roof.

Photographer: Dennis Gilbert/4518:40

ENGINEERING FACULTY, LEICESTER UNIVERSITY, LEICESTERSHIRE, ENGLAND (1963)

James Stirling and James Gowan

The last building designed by Stirling and Gowan, the Engineering Faculty building is an ensemble of parts drawing inspiration from far afield. The dominating tower overlooks the prism skylights of the workshops.

Photographer: (insert) Jeremy Cockayne/300:800, (main) Richard Einzig/300:20

Economist Buildings, London, England (1964)

Alison and Peter Smithson

Within their own piazza, a trio of small towers sits amongst the Georgian streets of central London. The Brutalism of previous work was carefully restrained in this sensitive area of London.

Photographer: Martin Jones/3268:30

PARK HILL AND HYDE PARK ESTATES, SHEFFIELD, YORKSHIRE, ENGLAND (1965)

J. L. Womersley and others

Based on the Le Corbusier's *Unités*, these blocks failed to live up to the ideological model. Designed around the principle of "Streets in the sky," times changed so did the occupiers' attitudes.

Photographer: Dennis Gilbert/7118:30

CENTRE POINT, LONDON, ENGLAND (1966)

Colonel Richard Seifert

The recently proposed listing for this much-maligned focal point of London's West End adds further to its tubulent story. The looming concrete lattice structure acts as a bookend to Tottenham Court Road.

Photographer: Dennis Gilbert/1666:70

MARINA CITY, CHICAGO, ILLINOIS, UNITED STATES (1967)

Bertrand Goldberg Associates

With an appearance that wouldn't feel out of place in the *Jetsons*, Marina City's twin towers present a surreal face to the river below. Each tower supports 40 floors of apartments on a spiralled carpark base; seen from any angle the towers retain their intended purity.

Photographer: Barry Edwards/5248:20

U.S. Pavilion at Expo '67, Montreal, Canada (1967)

Richard Buckminster Fuller

Always pushing the envelope of possibilities, Fuller created the Geodesic Domes; structures based upon octahedrons or tetrahedrons.

Photographer: Alex Bartel/3121:10

HABITAT HOUSING AT EXPO '67, MONTREAL, CANADA (1967)

Moshie Safdie

One of the most unusual housing developments, Habitat was Safdie's first major work, bringing him instant fame. A series of prefabricated boxes fit together to give everyone a roof garden, privacy and a unique view.

Photographer: Richard Bryant/687:10

STUDENT HOUSING, UNIVERSITY OF EAST ANGLIA, NORWICH, NORFOLK, ENGLAND (1968)

Denys Lasdun

A 20th century interpretation of a ziggurat, these accommodation blocks set out to provide spacious internal and external living facilities at a new university.

Photographer: Richard Einzig/5945:10

HAYWARD GALLERY, SOUTH BANK, LONDON, ENGLAND (1968)

LCC Architects Department

An uncompromising and unsuccessful attempt to realise the ideals of Le Corbusier and the Brutalist, the Hayward Gallery sits awkwardly on the South Bank. Its defensive nature adds to the continual problems of the South Bank and any potential redevelopment.

Photographer: Martin Jones/2101:20

Lake Point Tower, Chicago, Illinois, United States (1968)

Schipporeit-Heinrich Associates

The tower block was designed by former students of Mies van der Rohe, and is very reminiscent of Mies' 1921 glass tower. It has a clover-shaped plan.

Photographer: Barry Edwards/5249:10

NEUE NATIONALGALERIE, BERLIN, GERMANY (1968)

Ludwig Mies van der Rohe

The last major work by Mies, the gallery is the culmination of a series of pavilions and clearly demonstrates all of his basic principles. A giant oversized canopy, supported on eight recessed cruciform columns, encloses an open-plan exhibition space divided only by moveable partitions.

Photographer: Richard Bryant/466:10

CENTRAAL BEHEER, APELDOORN, NETHERLANDS (1972)

Herman Hertzberger

This office is comprised of a series of adjoining pavilions whose interior spaces open and close created views, vistas and balconies into voids. The dull interiors are given life by the introduction of internal planting within the voids.

Photographer: Richard Bryant/52:20

BRION CEMETERY, SAN VITO D'ALTIVOLE, NEAR TREVISO, ITALY (1972)

Carlo Scarpa

Keeping to the Italian tradition of great splendour in cemetery designs, Scarpa has envisaged an exquisite celebration of death.

Photographer: Stefan Buzas/3854:10

FINLANDIA HALL, HELSINKI, FINLAND (1972)

Alvar Aalto

Often described as national romanticism, Aalto style created a humane vernacular architecture inspired by his surroundings. His brand of Modernism still remains in favour long after many of his contemporaries.

Photographer: Richard Einzig/879:150

TRELLICK TOWER, WESTBOURNE PARK, LONDON, ENGLAND (1972)

Erno Goldfinger

This landmark structure in west London is a combination of the rational structure and the ideology of Le Corbusier's *Unités*. The double-aspect duplex apartments have long since become fashionable, offering spacious accommodation for the occupiers.

Photographer: David Churchill/4461:10

Barbican Centre, City of London, England (1973)

Chamberlin, Powell and Bon

Urban *mise-en-scène* characterises the work of this firm, and the Barbican Centre is testament to its ideals. Constructed with separate routes for traffic and pedestrians, the centre has an appearance of enclosure, but the interior opens up into small courtyards.

Photographer: Richard Einzig/880:50

WILLIS FABER AND DUMAS, IPSWICH, SUFFOLK, ENGLAND (1975)

Foster Associates

It is not until dusk draws in that this building starts to wake and display its inner secrets to the unsuspecting observer. The sleek black glass office block pushed the technical boundaries of the time, instantly creating higher standards for work environments.

Photographer: Richard Bryant/78:5

SYDNEY OPERA HOUSE, SYDNEY, AUSTRALIA (1973)

Jørn Utzon

Pre-cast concrete sections were fixed together to produce the outer shells, which were then clad in ceramic tiles that reflect the sky and water. Whether the form was inspired by turtles or sails, it is a unique icon. Unfortunately, the interiors lack the ambition and fluidity of the outer shells.

Photographer: Alan Williams/1249

The Las Veags Strip, Las Vegas, Nevada, United States (20th century)

The world renowned "City of Sin" could have only been built in America: where else would the gaudy Mecca of neon have been allowed. Now altered due to large corporations' investments, the old strip sits warm in our hearts, evoking thoughts of gangsters and the *Rockford Files*.

Photographer: Alex Bartel/2979:30

WALDEN 7, ST. JUST DESVERN, BARCELONA, SPAIN (1975)

Taller De Arquitectura (Richard Bofill)

Resembling something Franz Kafka would find welcoming, this huge apartment block has surreal qualities with no apparent logic. For many years the tiles of this brutal and intimidating concrete block would fall to earth: Kafka would relish such details.

Photographer: Prisma/4621:40

National Theatre, South Bank, London, England (1975)

Denys Lasdun

With its back to the sun, the theatre's stepped façade of terraces and flytowers sits at the heart of the problematic South Bank complex. The exterior is saved by the quality of the interior spaces and attention to detail in the three theatres.

Photographer: Richard Bryant/651:160

The Baylis Terrace
PEPSI
Box Office

POMPIDOU CENTRE, PARIS, FRANCE (1977)

Renzo Piano and Richard Rogers

The epitome of High-Tech, the Pompidou achieves the desire of maximum floor space by placing the structural components, vertical circulation and services on the outside. A better example of a building showing its internal works cannot be found.

Photographer: Paul Raftery/290:410

CHURCH AT RIOLA DI VERGATO, NEAR BOLOGNA, ITALY (1978)

Alvar Aalto

Completed after his death in 1976 by his architect wife Elissa Makiniemi, Riola has a serene simplicity and purity about its design. The use of chairs rather than pews adds to the simplicity.

Photographer: Richard Einzig/878:20

SAINSBURY CENTRE, UNIVERSITY OF EAST ANGLIA, NORWICH, NORFOLK, ENGLAND (1977)

Foster Associates

As sheds go, few are as pristine as this; clad in white aluminium panels over steel trusses, the interior space is uninterrupted by the technical bits and pieces. Foster used the voids in the trusses to stuff all the building's workings out of sight, thus leaving unsullied the artworks that occupy the building.

Photographer: Jeremy Cockayne/75:350

Speelhuis Housing Estate, Helmond, Rotterdam, Netherlands (1978)

Piet Blom

The dominant theme in this estate is simple and striking: accommodation that fits into cubes twisted onto their corners. Each cube is support on a hexagonal shaft, giving the impression of a Cubist view of a "forest."

Photographer: Alex Bartel/779:150

Byker Wall, Newcastle-upon-Tyne, England (1979)

Ralph Erskine

As in many working class areas across Britain, the undeveloped proposals for large motorways created responsive housing schemes, none better than Byker Wall. An eight-storey wall encloses the urban village; the estate's potential residents were allowed to participate in the design process, culminating in a friendly and very successful public housing scheme.

Photographer: Colin Dixon/4741:10

Garden Grove Community Church (Crystal Cathedral), Los Angeles, California, United States (1980)

Philip Johnson and John Burgee

Technically brilliant — a space-frame clad in its entirety in reflective glass, basking the congregation in the warm West Coast sun. Thousands can worship in this cavernous structure that displays an ostentatious opulence on a scale rarely seen, and rarely permitted.

Photographer: Richard Bryant/359:10

THE WHITE HOUSE (PARLIAMENT BUILDING) MOSCOW, RUSSIA (1981)

The authoritarian nature of many buildings constructed during the Cold War clearly demonstrates the social straightjacketing that Government wielded. Standing on the banks of the River Moskva, the new Parliament building demonstrates the complete communist dogma.

Photographer: Alan Williams/5711:20

AT&T Building, New York City, New York, United States (1982)

Philip Johnson and John Burgee

Post-Modernism was all about taking what you wanted, discarding what was surplus and the great architectural jokes. A split pediment office block adorned in pink granite started a disconcerting trend only the 1980s could have produced.

Photographer: Richard Bryant/1281:10

Triton Hotel, Ahungala, Sri Lanka (1983)

Geoffrey Bawa

Renowned for combining traditional symbolism with modern techniques, the hotel has the appearance of a traditional regional vernacular building. The encroachment of the surrounding natural environment makes the hotel memorable.

Photographer: Richard Bryant/515:20

Sri Lankan Parliament, Columbo, Sri Lanka (1983)

From across the lake it is not apparent that the design was compromised by the contractor's construction schedule. Bawa's signature of attention to detail was not allowed to flourish.

Photographer: Richard Bryant/513:110

House at Glenorie, North Sydney, Australia (1985)

Glen Murcutt

Evocative of the traditional settlers' vernacular, Murcutt has combined this with his own brand of Modernism in a sparse suburb of North Sydney. With its simple and well throughout plan, the house overcomes many problems associated with its environment.

Photographer: Richard Bryant/57:20

Neue Staatsgalerie, Stuttgart, Germany (1984)

James Stirling and Michael Wilford

Designed to be part of the city, pedestrian routes run through the heart of the gallery. Stirling and Wilford mixed and matched styles to create one of the buildings of the 1980s. Stirling's interpretation of Classicism manifested itself in details of the highest quality and finishes. The Staats was an early example of the importance of galleries and museums to the development of architecture in the late 20th century.

Photographer: Richard Bryant/47

STAATSGALERIE

DE MENIL ART GALLERY, HOUSTON, TEXAS, UNITED STATES (1986)

Renzo Piano Building Workshop

A basic concept of viewing the exhibits almost entirely in natural daylight led to the solution provided by the light baffles that trademark the gallery. Elegantly simple in execution, the Menil provides evidence that high-tech solutions can work on a small scale effectively.

Photographer: Richard Bryant/156:90

LLOYDS OF LONDON, CITY OF LONDON, ENGLAND (1986)

Richard Rogers

Destined to be the building for which Rogers will be best remembered, Lloyds made a huge impact in the conservative City of London. The sleek high-tech cathedral to money still baffles Londoners and visitors alike with its entrails visible for all to see; surely the toilets cannot be bolted to the outside?

Photographer: Richard Bryant/106:480

Hong Kong and Shanghai Bank, Hong Kong (1986)

Foster Associates

A staggering investment was required to build this grand exo-skeletal banking house that crowned the British high-tech age. Open-planned floors weere realised by pushing the services and circulation to the envelope's extremities.

Photographer: Ian Lambot/64:300

MOUND STAND, LORD'S CRICKET GROUND, LONDON, ENGLAND (1987)

Michael Hopkins

Borrowing from the lessons learned from his earlier work on the Schlumberger Research Laboratories; Hopkins used fabric to create a series of tented peaks to cover the stand. Tensile cables are used to keep the fabric in tension supported by six cruciform masts.

Photographer: Richard Bryant/174:70

VITRA MUSEUM, WEIL-AM-RHEIN, GERMANY (1988)

Frank O. Gehry

Gehry's first major commission in Europe was, appropriately enough, a building to display the wonders of designer furniture. The resultant pavilion shows the eccentricity that Gehry is famed for; unusual angles, sweeping curves and fragmented façades.

Photographer: Richard Bryant/794:290

L'INSTITUT DU MONDE ARABE, PARIS, FRANCE (1988)

Jean Nouvel

One of President Mitterand's *Grand Projects* for Paris, the institute is famed for its south-facing façade of glass blocks in a steel frame work. This wall controls the amount of direct sunlight entering the building and is a clever demonstration of technology as art, as architecture.

Photographer: Stephane Couturier/589

KIDOSAKI HOUSE, TOKYO, JAPAN (1987)

Tadao Ando

From the street the house appearsunwelcoming. The paradigm was to introduce as much light as possible whilst retaining privacy. Detailed to precision, the exposed concrete walls are the canvases for which Ando allows the sun to create the drama of the space.

Photographer: Richard Bryant/217:10

MUSEUM OF CIVILISATION, OTTAWA, CANADA (1988)

Douglas Cardinal

Mainly devoted to the Native North Americans, this museum draws on relics of their culture to create the main forms and features. The roofs are reminiscent of canoe hulls, while the entrances are inspired by the totem pole.

Photographer: Richard Bryant/686:40

SAINSBURY GALLERY, NATIONAL GALLERY, LONDON, ENGLAND (1987)

Venturi, Scott-Brown

The outcome of the unsolicited intervention by the Prince of Wales, the extension for the National is a compromise and not what it should have been: a potential masterpiece within the most popular London square. Classical references and architectural jokes are all we are left to view; thankfully the art overwhelms the interiors.

Photographer: Richard Bryant/1539:260

Pumping Station, Docklands, London, England (1988)

John Outram

A box whose decorations far and away exceed the functions of its contents, this pumping station on the River Thames draws on classical and nautical inspirations.

Photographer: Richard Bryant/557:10

Richmond Riverside, Richmond-upon-Thames, Surrey, England (1988)

Quinlan Terry

The riverside office, shop and restaurant complex appears to the layman to be a faithful reproduction of Georgian architecture. However, peeling the façades away shows a heavy reliance on modern building techniques and services.

Photographer: David Churchill/710:10

PYRAMID, THE LOUVRE, PARIS, FRANCE (1989)

I. M. Pei

Descending via a spiral staircase into the spacious subterranean lobby, the real cleverness of the Louvre's entrance pyramid becomes apparent.

Photographer: Stephane Couturier/443:50

PYRAMID, THE LOUVRE, PARIS, FRANCE (1989)

I. M. Pei

After all the fuss, another of Paris's *Grand Projects*, the pyramid at the Louvre, is a much-loved addition to the city. The entrance to the lower level spaces, Pie uses an efficient structural system to create the glass sides.

Photographer: Malcolm Dixon/443:310

Parc de la Villette, Paris, France (1989)

Bernard Tschumi

The park — made up of a series of follies painted bright red, the deconstructionist's chosen hue — has never quite lived up to expectations.

Photographer: Richard Bryant/442:80

HAAS HAUS, VIENNA, AUSTRIA (1990)

Hans Hollein

In a sensitive Viennese site, opposite St Stephen's, one of Europe's best cathedrals, Hollein designed a reflective glass-cylinder department store and offices.

Photographer: Richard Bryant/ 1182:130

CHIAT DAY HEADQUARTERS, VENICE BEACH, SANTA MONICA, CALIFORNIA, UNITED STATES (1990)

Frank O. Gehry

Famous for the Claes Oldenburg's binoculars, which dominate the façade, the Chiat Day headquarters use imagery of the past and present; the yacht and the trees.

Photographer: John Edward Linden/4704:40

THE WALLED CITY, KOWLOON, HONG KONG (1990S)

Derived from the basic need for shelter, this renowned shantytown was a labyrinth. Now demolished, the Wall City was evidence of natural growth and development out of necessity.

Photographer: Ian Lambot/4314:10

WESTIN REGINA HOTEL, BAJA, MEXICO (1990)

Javier Sordo Madaleno

The simplistic forms at this resort hotel have characteristics that can be found in both traditional and modern Mexican architecture. A mixture of textures and bold colours gives the architecture a distinctive personality that evokes memories of recent architects such as Barragn.

Photographer: Natalie Tepper/7537:50

In-N-Out Burger Restaurant, Westwood, Los Angeles, United States (1990)

In 1948, Harry and Esther Snyder in Baldwin Park founded the first "In-N-Out" drive-thru hamburger stand where customers could order through a two-way speaker box without leaving their car. The aesthetics typify the local modern vernacular of L.A. — Pop-Architecture.

Photographer: John Edward Linden/8758:60

LA GRANDE ARCHE, LA DÉFENSE, PARIS, FRANCE (1990)

Johann Otto von Spreckelsen

One of the most recognised of Mitterand's *Grand Projects*; the Arche sits at the end of the axis from the Arc de Triomphe. The 328ft hollow cube arch houses 35 floors of government offices behind its white marble and glass façades. At the base of the Arche, under a tensile fabric tent, lies the glass entrance and the access point to the lifts.

Photographer: John Edward Linden/662:140

HAMBURG FERRY AND CRUISE SHIP TERMINAL, HAMBURG-ALTONA, GERMANY (1990)

Alsop and Lyle Architects

Located on the River Elbe, the terminal incorporates the longest office block in Europe at 1,640ft. Visual references to the history of the river and sea are present, reminders of its past importance to the city.

Photographer: John Edward Linden/8011:10

Neuendorf House, Mallorca, Spain (1990)

John Pawson and Claudio Silvestrin

One of the few truly designed minimal houses of the world, this holiday house is a carefully thought-out exploration of light and shadow. A simple composition of stone, wood and concrete, the house is introverted, except for the lap pool, which stretches out into the surrounding fields.

Photographer: Richard Bryant/876

CANARY WHARF TOWER, DOCKLANDS, LONDON, ENGLAND (1991)

Cesar Pelli

Briefly the tallest building in Europe at 803.8ft, the tower carries with it the stigma attached from the development's troubled start. Rising out of a bland Post-modern development, the tower is reminiscent of the architect's previous towers in Battery Park, New York.

Photographer: Richard Bryant/2332:10

Kunst- und Ausstellungshalle, Bonn, Germany (1992)

Gustav Peichl

The usual characteristics of Peichl — machine aesthetics — have given way to a purer Modernist architecture. The striking feature of the museum is the conical skylights on the roof.

Photographer: Richard Bryant/ 3105:110

POUNDBURY VILLAGE (PHASE 1), DORCHESTER, DORSET, ENGLAND (1992)

Leon Krier and others

An unsuccessful attempt to recreate the idyllic village of yesteryear, this development in the backwoods of England was to be the new model for living, with a royal seal of approval.

Photographer: Joe Low/5551:60

THE ARK, HAMMERSMITH, LONDON, ENGLAND (1992)

Ralph Erskine

An unusual office block that responds to its urban setting, the Ark's design intentions, like many of Erskine's other works, has the user at the forefront.

Photographer: Mark Fiennes/3109:270

Opéra de Lyon, Lyon, France (1993)

Jean Nouvel

Hollowing out the original building by Chenavard and Pollet (1831), Nouvel has managed to triple the interior volume. Lighting specialist Yann Kersalë gives Nouvel's 65½ft high cylindrical roof extension its distinctive red glow.

Photographer: Alex Bartel/3962:200

Crédit Lyonais (The Boot), Euralille complex, Lille, France (1993)

Christian de Portzamparc

Within the Euralille complex, master plan by Office of Modern Architecture , de Portzamparc designed the unusual boot-like-office.

Photographer: John Edward Linden/5252:110

Satolas TGV Station, Lyon-Satolas, France (1993)

Santiago Calatrava

The bird-like concourse of the train terminal echoes Eero Saarinen's TWA Terminal at JFK Airport. The 1,640ft long platforms that sit either side of two through lines were specially constructed to withstand the "shock waves" of the 186mph TGV trains.

Photographer: Paul Raftery/4836:10

Supreme Court, Jerusalem, Israel (1993)

Ram Karmi and Ada Karmi-Melamede

Basking in the Mediterranean sun, the Supreme Court complex rises like an ancient ziggurat of the region. Controlling the climate plays a key role in the design process, maintaining workable conditions in an extreme climate.

Photographer: Richard Bryant/3370:800

SUPREME COURT, JERUSALEM, ISRAEL (1993)

Ram Karmi and Ada Karmi-Melamede

The exquisite detailing and motifs owe equally to the region as a whole rather than just the Modernism ideology.

Photographer: Richard Bryant/3370:200

Torre de Collserola, Barcelona, Spain (1994)

Sir Norman Foster and Partners

Standing as tall as the Eiffel Tower, with a public viewing platform high above the ground, this communication tower accurately reflects its high-tech purpose. The mast balances precariously on the mountainside, held in true by three triads of guy wires.

Photographer: Richard Bryant/3112:130

FOUNDATION CARTIER, PARIS, FRANCE (1994)

Jean Nouvel

Residing behind a series of screens that could past for scaffolding, the museum central themes are transparency and a connection with nature. The effect is of a building that is as unobtrusive as possible.

Photographer: John Edward Linden/4618:70

FUJI TELEVISION BUILDING, FUJI BROADCASTING, TOKYO, JAPAN (1994)

Kenzo Tange Associates

Modern Japanese architecture has tended to produce monuments rather than substance, in a mix of recent styles incorporating high technology. This heroic building by Tange, who has always been a major influence in Japan, is in Tokyo's Docklands.

Photographer: William Tingey/8031:80

Opéra de la Bastille, Paris, France (1994)

Carlos Ott

The first opera house to be built in Paris in a hundred years, the Bastille heralds a departure from the Classical forms typified in the Garnier's Opera House.

Photographer: Richard Bryant/637:30

Tokyo Big Sight, International Exhibition Hall, Tokyo, Japan (1994)

Sato Sogokeikau

Another part of the redevelopment of Tokyo's Docklands, the Exhibition Hall, displays the bold composition of forms characteristic of modern Japan.

Photographer: William Tingey/8030:90

HÔTEL DU DÉPARTMENT, MARSEILLE, FRANCE (1994)

William Alsop Architects

Alsop's first major commission was this regional government headquarters; a bold ultramarine aerodynamic building that contrasts greatly with the surrounding tiled roofs.

Photographer: Paul Raftery/3907:350

Bibliothèque Nationale, Paris, France (1995)

Dominique Perrault

The four giant open book towers that distinguish the library have had their fair share of problems, not least the storage of the books in the towers. At great expense new wooden louvers were installed to protect the precious stock.

Photographer: Paul Raftery/5422:20

SUNTEC CITY, SINGAPORE (1996)

Tsao & McKown Architects

The largest exhibition centre in Southeast Asia, the development was completed prior to the collapse in the Pacific Rim economy. It displays the clean aesthetics seen in the company's domestic work, with a variety of differing textures and materials.

Photographer: Richard Bryant/7441:230

EUROPEAN COURT OF HUMAN RIGHTS, STRASBOURG, FRANCE (1995)

Richard Rogers and Partners

Designed around the notion of the bi-partie function of organisation, which has now changed in favour of a unique court structure; the courts are a rational solution to the function's complexity. Central to the design is the glazed entrance rotunda with adjoining court chambers.

Photographer: Paul Raftery/5500:130

LINGOTTO CONFERENCE CENTRE, TURIN, ITALY (1996)

Renzo Piano Building Workshop

Giacomo Mattë-Trucco's Fiat Factory (1923), that included the famous racetrack on the roof, has been converted and refurbished by Piano. The most obvious addition is the futuristic glass orb meeting room perched at one end of the racetrack, peering out over the city.

Photographer: Paul Raftery/8008:70

INTERNATIONAL FORUM, TOKYO, JAPAN (1996)

Rafael Vinoly

Responding to the site's shape and the client's wishes, independent auditoriums were established, isolated from the adjacent railway lines by a great glass void. A sleek glazed wedge hall — the Glass Hall, with its bow-like roof — acts as an orientation space for the rest of the complex.

Photographer: John Edward Linden/8251

British Library, St. Pancras, London, England (1997)

Twenty-three years in the making, the new British Library has recently opened, but the delay in construction anchors its style in the recent past. The need for a new home for the nation's books — 200 miles of shelving in the basement — allowed for the first time accurately controlled atmospheric conditions.

Photographer: Richard Bryant/8300:20

River and Rowing Museum, Henley-on-Thames, England (1997)

David Chipperfield Architects

Renowned for numerous shops and restaurants, Chipperfield needed to transform the strict aesthetics he had developed over the years for the purpose-built museum. A careful selection of materials reflects the traditions of the river culture.

Photographer: Richard Bryant/7582:20

SWAMINARAYAN HINDU TEMPLE, NEASDEN, LONDON, ENGLAND (1997 AD)

One of the largest Hindu temples outside Asia, its white marble was cut and shaped mainly in India and shipped to England. Hindu religious details and motifs have been applied: this is no pastiche on Hindu architecture, and has the heritage and craftsmanship of tradition.

Photographer: David Churchill/5856:10

PETRONAS TOWERS, KUALA LUMPUR, MALAYSIA (1997)

Cesar Pelli

The 88-storey, 451m towers are joined by a sky bridge, and when completed took the mantle as the world's tallest building.

Photographer: Richard Bryant/8000:180

PETRONAS TOWERS, KUALA LUMPUR, MALAYSIA (1997)

Cesar Pelli

A symbol of the success of the Pacific Rim, the twin towers of K.L., though based firmly in the technology of the late 20th century, draws architectural inspiration from Buddhist temples.

Photographer: Richard Bryant/8000:180

THE AMERICAN AIR MUSEUM IN BRITAIN, DUXFORD, CAMBRIDGESHIRE, ENGLAND (1997)

Sir Norman Foster and Partners

Based around the need to house the giant American Boeing B-52 Stratofortress bomber, Foster has created a modern aircraft hanger whose intrusion in the landscape is kept to a minimum. A departure from the high-tech serviced buildings, Duxford has no environmental services relying solely on the materials chosen.

Photographer: Richard Bryant/8246:90

Sto Building K, Weizen, Bravaria Germany (1997)

Michael Wilford and Partners

Marking a clear change in direction for the office once headed by James Stirling, Sto Building K gives the impression of lightness and elegance, without overpowering the landscape. The oval entrance rises into the offset offices with dramatic effect.

Photographer: Richard Bryant: 8445:30

YAMANASHI FRUIT MUSEUM AND GARDEN, YAMANASHI, JAPAN (1997)

Itsuko Hasegawa Atelier

On a hillside above the Fuefuki River, in an area famous for agriculture, lie three steel, glass and concrete structures resembling fruit and seeds surrounded by public gardens. These incorporate a greenhouse, an event space and restaurant/gift shop as well as the workshops for the maintenance of the vegetation.

Photographer: John Edward Linden/8250:40

GUGGENHEIM MUSEUM, BILBAO, SPAIN (1998)

Frank O. Gehry

Gehry's most prominent finished commission to date, the Guggenheim is a spectacular titanium-clad exploration of space. The Guggenheim in Bilbao epitomises the change of direction within architecture: museums are now the new cathedrals and no expense is spared in their construction. Large-scale temporary exhibitions can be housed in the 100ft wide by 426ft long gallery.

Photographer: Paul Raftery/8501

No.1 Poultry, City of London, England (1998)

James Stirling and Michael Wilford

Encompassing offices, shops, restaurants and a roof garden, this ship-like structure dominates the attention of the area.

Photographer: Richard Bryant/8510:10

No.1 Poultry, City of London, England (1998)

James Stirling and Michael Wilford

Built on the site of the old Mappin and Webb building, No. 1 Poultry, after years of political bickering, has finally been completed. Constructed several years after Stirling's death all the usual Post-modern tricks are employed.

Photographer: Richard Bryant/8510:240

THE GETTY CENTER, LOS ANGELES, CALIFORNIA, UNITED STATES (1998)

Richard Meier

They say "art is the new religion": this is has never been better shown than at the Getty Center which sits proudly high on a hill overlooking the urban sprawl. Meier's usual pristine white exteriors have been compromised by the wishes of the client's insistence for travertine.

Photographer: John Edward Linden/8515:440

THE GETTY CENTER, LOS ANGELES, CALIFORNIA, UNITED STATES (1998)

Richard Meier

At a staggering one billion dollars construction cost, and more spent on the artworks to fill the galleries, the Getty Center is a series of pavilions set amongst beautifully sculptured gardens.

Photographer: John Edward Linden/8515:30

Jewish Museum, Berlin, Germany (1999)

Daniel Libeskind

Few buildings have been so eagerly awaited as Libeskind's Jewish Museum; a zigzag zinc-clad composition, beside the old Berlin Museum.

Photographer: Richard Bryant/8611:30

NATIONAL CENTRE FOR POPULAR MUSIC, SHEFFIELD, YORKSHIRE, ENGLAND (1999)

Branson Coates

Four steel drums house the exhibition spaces linked by a cruciform circulation/orientation route. It is the first free-standing building, constructed from scratch, by Branson Coates in this country.

Photographer: Martine Hamilton Knight/9053:60

Tate Gallery of Modern Art, Bankside, London, England (2000 AD)

Herzog De Meuron

On a prime site on the banks of the Thames, the Tate is converting an old power station to house part of its vast collection. The new gallery will be linked to the City of London via Norman Foster's Millennium Bridge.

Photographer: Richard Glover/4020:100

MILLENNIUM DOME, GREENWICH PENINSULA, LONDON, ENGLAND (2000)

Richard Rogers Partnership

Twelve angled masts, evoking memories of Powell and Moya's Skylon at the 1951 Festival of Britain, support the double-layered Teflon roof. For the cost of its construction, it is said that a dozen of Gehry's Guggenheims could have been built.

Photographer: Richard Bryant/8587:180

MILLENNIUM DOME, GREENWICH PENINSULA, LONDON, ENGLAND (2000)

Richard Rogers Partnership

Occupying a large disused industrial site, the one kilometre circumference dome is the centrepiece for Britain's millennium celebrations. The success of the controversial dome will not be known for many years.

Photographer: Richard Bryant/8587:160

WARNING

INDEX